Ed's ROTTENEST SONGS EVER

Sing along with Ed

Ed's

HOTEST
ROTTENEST
RUGBY
&
BAWDY BALLADS

They were Rotten once
and they still are!
ENJOY!

ISBN 978-0-9809255-9-3

NOTICE

Some of these ballads are course and vulgar. They are sung at your own risk. I take no responsibility for the outcome, the laughs, the scorn or the aggression that may arise from the use of this "Adult" material. These Ballads are taken from the worst military, rugby, bar and back room songs written.

This song book is provided for private use and is a compilation of the best (worst) of my favorite songs. I compiled them for my own use and simply use reatespace to print them for me. All material has been taken from the public domain off the Internet and the book is not meant for commercial use. If you happen to wander here, and want a copy, you are simply paying for printing cost. It is for your private fun and enjoyment and I do not guarantee the accuracy of the chords, words or material. I do guarantee, however, that these songs when sung in the right place (whatever that is) will give you fun and laughs.

Ed Rychkun

www.edrychkun.com

1. A RUGBY TOAST

(Toast)

Here's to America,
Land of the wuss.
Where one in the hand,
Is worth two in the bush.
But the girls all say,
If you can make it stand,
A push in the bush is worth two in the hand!

2 A SONG ABOUT TURDS

CHORUS: Toorala, Tooralay,
A rolling stone gathers no moss so they say;
Sing along with the birds
It's a beautiful song but it's all about turds.

There was an old lady who lived on West Street,
And she was all stopped up from too much to eat,
So she swallowed some pills without reading the box,
And the first thing she knew turds came flying like rocks.

She ran to the window and stuck out her ass,
Just as she did a young cowboy did pass,
He turned to the sound that he heard up on high,
And a bloody great turd hit him right in the eye.

He ran to the east and he ran to the west,
A bloody great turd hit him right in the chest.
He ran to the north and he ran to the south,
Another great turd hit him right in the mouth.

If ever you pass o'er the Flat River Bridge,
And see a young cowboy asleep on the ridge,
Just stop by the roadside and pray for a bit,
Drop a tear for a cowboy who is buried in shit.

3. A TOAST TO BEER

(Toast)

If I had a dog that could piss this stuff
And I was sure that dog could piss enough
I'd tie his head to the foot of my bed
And such his dick 'til we both dropped dead.

4. A TOAST TO MADGE

(Toast)

("Madge" is replaced by the name of the woman you want to honor.)

Here's to Madge, that filthy bitch
Whose cunt is lined with seven year itch
Green matter oozes between her toes
Filthy corruption flows through her nose.

Yet before I climb those scaly thighs
And suck those crusty tits
I'd rather drink a quart of buzzard's piss
And swim the River Shits.

Oh cunt, oh cunt, thy deep and bottomless])it
All matted with hair and covered with shit
Like a pole cat's ass that smellest so bad
Oh cunt, oh cunt, thou must be had.

5. A TOAST TO THE LADIES

(Toast)

Here's to the breezes that blow through the treeses
That lifts the girls' chemises above their kneeses
To show us what pleases, and teases, and squeezes
And gives us venereal diseases, By Jesus!

6. ABORTION

(Sung to the tune of "Jadda")

Abortion, Abortion, A-B-O-R-T-I-O-N (Ba-Bum, Bum, Bum)
Abortion, Abortion, A-B-O-R-T-I-O-N (Ba-Bum, Bum, Bum)
Well you get that poker nice and hot,
Then you shove it way up in her twat.
Oh Abortion, Abortion, A-B-O-R-T-I-O-N (Ba-Bum, Bum,
Bum)

Abortion, Abortion, A-B-O-R-T-I-O-N (Ba-Bum, Bum, Bum)
Abortion, Abortion, A-B-O-R-T-I-O-N (Ba-Bum, Bum, Bum)
Sticks and coat hangers and all the rest,
But I like Drano, it ' s the best.
Oh Abortion, Abortion, A-B-O-R-T-I-O-N (Ba-Bum, Bum,
Bum)

Baby Fuck, Baby Fuck, B-A-B-Y F-U-C-K (Ba-Bum, Bum,
Bum)
Baby Fuck, Baby Fuck, B-A-B-Y F-U-C-K (Ba-Bum, Bum,
Bum)
First you throw the baby on the bed,
And then you fuck the soft spot in its head.
Oh Baby Fuck, Baby Fuck, B-A-B-Y F-U-C-K (Ba-Bum, Bum,
Bum)

Blow Job, Blow Job, B-L-O-W J-O-B (Ba-Bum, Bum, Bum)
Blow Job, Blow Job, B-L-O-W J-O-B (Ba-Bum, Bum, Bum)
Eastside, westside, northside, south,
My baby likes it best when I cum in her mouth.
Oh Blow Job, Blow Job, B-L-O-W J-O-B (Ba-Bum, Bum,
Bum)

Bum Fuck, Bum Fuck, B-U-M F-U-C-K (Ba-Bum, Bum, Bum)
Bum Fuck, Bum Fuck, B-U-M F-U-C-K (Ba-Bum, Bum, Bum)
Eastside, westside, northside, down,
My baby likes it best when I cum in her brown.
Bum Fuck, Bum Fuck, B-U-M F-U-C-K (Ba-Bum, Bum, Bum)

Dirtbag, Dirtbag, D-I-R-T-B-A-G (Ba-Bum, Bum, Bum)
Dirtbag, Dirtbag, D-I-R-T-B-A-G (Ba-Bum, Bum, Bum)
They may be fat and they may be thin,
But - they 're all beauty queens when you get it in.
Dirtbag Dirtbag, D-I-R-T-B-A-G (Ba-Bum, Bum, Bum)

Hand Job , Hand Job, H-A-N-D J-O-B (Ba-Bum, Bum, Bum)
Hand Job, Hand Job, H-A-N-D J-O-B (Ba-Bum, Bum, Bum)
You wrap your hand around your gland,
You slap it around 'til it just won't stand.
Hand Job, Hand Job, H-A-N-D J-O-B (Ba-Bum, Bum, Bum)

Muff Dive, Muff Dive, M-U-F-F D-I-V-E (Ba-Bum, Bum, Bum)
Muff Dive, Muff Dive, M-U-F-F D-I-V-E (Ba-Bum, Bum, Bum)
She wraps her legs around your face,
You lick and slobber all over the place.
Muff Dive, Muff Dive, M-U-F-F D-I-V-E (Ba-Bum, Bum, Bum)

Poop Shoot, Poop Shoot, P-O-O-P S-H-O-O-T (Ba-Bum, Bum,
Bum
Poop Shoot, Poop Shoot, P-O-O-P S-H-O-O-T (Ba-Bum, Bum,
Bum)
Back door, cornhole, it's a gas,
You ram that pecker right up her ass.
Poop Shoot, Poop Shoot, P-O-O-P S-H-O-O-T (Ba-Bum, Bum,
Bum)

Scrotum, Scrotum, S-C-R-O-T-U-M (Ba-Bum, Bum, Bum)
Scrotum, Scrotum, S-C-R-O-T-U-M (Ba-Bum, Bum, Bum)
Well it's mangey, rangey, and covered with hair,
But what would you do if it wasn't there?
Scrotum, Scrotum, S-C-R-O-T-U-M (Ba-Bum, Bum, Bum)
I really mean it, S-C-R-O-T-U-M.

Smegma, Smegma, S-M-E-G-M-A (Ba-Bum, Bum, Bum
Smegma, Smegma, S-M-E-G-M-A (Ba-Bum, Bum, Bum)
It's white and cheesy, and it smells like taint,
But if you eat too much, you're liable to faint.
Smegma, Smegma, S-M-E-G-M-A (Ba-Bum, Bum, Bum)

Sodomy, Sodomy, S-O-D-O-M-Y (Ba-Bum, Bum, Bum)
Sodomy, Sodomy, S-O-D-O-M-Y (Ba-Bum, Bum, Bum)
you put the sheep's legs inside your boots,
so she won't change her mind when you're about to shoot.
so domy, Sodomy, S-O-D-O-M-Y (Ba-Bum, Bum, Bum)

Swallow, Swallow, S-W-A-L-L-O-W (Ba-Bum, Bum, Bum)
Swallow, Swallow, S-W-A-L-L-O-W (Ba-Bum, Bum, Bum)
She'll swallow it all and she'll swallow it well,
She'll swallow it all 'cause she ain't on the pill.
Swallow, Swallow, S-W-A-L-L-O-W (Ba-Bum, Bum, Bum)

Taint, Taint, T-A-i-N-T (Ba-Bum, Bum, Bum)
Taint, Taint, T-A-I-N-T (Ba-Bum, Bum, Bum)
It's not the ass and it's not the cunt,
It's the little bit of heaven 'tween the rear and the front.
Taint, Taint, T-A-I-N-T (Ba-Bum, Bum, Bum)

Tit Fuck, Tit Fuck, T-I-T F-U-C-K Ba-Bum, Bum, Bum)
Tit Fuck, Tit Fuck, T-I-T F-U-C-K (Ba-Bum, Bum, Bum)
Northside, southside, eastside, west,
My baby likes it best when I cum on her chest.
Oh Tit Fuck, Tit Fuck, T-I-T F-U-C-K (Ba-Bum, Bum, Bum)

Titties, Titties, T-I-T-T-I-E-S (Ba-Bum, Bum, Bum
Titties, Titties, T-I-T-T-I-E-S (Ba-Bum, Bum, Bum)
Well their just a part of the epiderm,
But I like 'em best when they're big and firm.
Titties, Titties, T-I-T-T-I-E-S (Ba-Bum, Bum, Bum)

7. ALL QUEERS TOGETHER

The sexual life of a camel, is stranger than anyone thinks,
At the height of the mating season,
He tries to bugger the sphinx,
But the sphinx with the wisdom of Allah,
Fills his arse with the sands from the Nile,
Which accounts for the hump on the camel,

And the sphinxs' inscrutable smile.

1st Chorus ;
 Singing Bum Titty, Bum Titty, Titty Bum,
 Bum Titty Bum Titty ay,
 Singing, Bum Titty, Bum Titty, Titty Bum,
 Singing, Bum Titty Bum Titty ay.

Now the sexual life of an Ostrich, is hard to understand,
We know this remarkable creature,
Will bury his head in the sand,
When another one comes up behind it,
And sees his great arse in the air,
Does he up with his chopper and grind it,
Or doesn't he fucking well care.
 1st Chorus

Oh, recent researches at Oxford, confirmed by Huxley and
all,
Conclusively prove that the hedgehog,
Cannot be buggered at all,
Oh why don't they do it at Oxford,
The same way they do it at Yale,
When they successfully bugger the hedgehog,
By shaving the hairs off its tail.
 1st Chorus

Oh, I went for a ride on a chuff-chuff,
There was hardly room to stand,
A little boy offered me his seat,
So I grabbed it with both my hands,

2nd Chorus ;
 Cos we're all queers together,
 That's why we go round in pairs,
 Yes we're all queers together,
 Excuse us while we go upstairs.

Oh, what do you want said the waiter, pensively picking his
nose,
Two hard boiled eggs you old bastard,
You can't stick your fingers in those,
 2nd Chorus

Oh, my name is Cecil, I live in Leicester Square,
I walks down Piccadilly, with a rose-bud in my hair,
 2nd Chorus

Oh, my is Basil, my friends name is Bond,
We're always together, they call us Basildon-Bond,
 2nd Chorus

'Twas Christmas night in the harem,
The Eunuchs were standing there,
Watching the fair young maidens, combing their pubic hair,
When the voice from the Sultan
Came echoing through the hall,
Saying what do you want for Christmas,
And the Eunuchs all answered BALLS.
 2nd Chorus

8. ALL THE NICE GIRLS LOVE A CANDLE

(Ship Ahoy)

All the nice girls love a candle,
All the nice girls love a wick,
For there's something about a candle
Which reminds them of a prick.
Nice and greasy, slips in easy,
It's a young girl's pride and joy,
Just to walk along the front,
With a candle up her cunt.
Ship ahoy girls, ship ahoy.

9. ALOUETTE

(Sung to the tune of "Alouette")

CHORUS: Alouette, gentille Alouette.
             Alouette, gentille plumerai.

(Start with chorus first and insert it between each verse.)

Leader: Does she have the scraggly hair?
Group: Yes, she has the scraggly hair.
Leader: Scraggly hair.
Group: Scraggly hair.
Leader: Alouette.
Group: Alouette.
Leader: OH!

Leader: Does she have the furrowed brow?
Group: Yes, she has the furrowed brow.
Leader: Furrowed brow.
Group: Furrowed brow.
Leader: Scraggly hair.
group: Scraggly hair.
Leader: Alouette.
Group: Alouette.
Leader: OH!

(Continue in this fashion, adding the current descriptive
phrase and then repeating all previous descriptive phrases.)

Two glass eyes?
Broken nose?
Two capped teeth?
Double chin?
Swinging tits?
Pot belly?
Clammy thighs?
Furry thing?

10. ANTHONY CLAIRE

CHORUS: For they were large balls, large balls,
                Twice as heavy as lead.
                With a dexterous twist of his muscular wrist,
                He threw them right over his head.

Now, there once was a man called Anthony Clair
He was a very fine jugulaire,
There wasn't a man who could compare
With the way he fiddled and played with his balls.

Now, Anthony was walking down the street,
Just by chance he happened to meet,
A pretty young maid with a dog at her feet,
Watching him fiddle and play with his balls.

Now, Anthony swung 'em round and round,
Let 'em go with a hell of a bound,
Right on the head of the faithful hound,
Watching him fiddle and play with his balls.

Now, the maiden, she was overwrought,
Swore she'd take the case to court,
For in her opinion no man ought
To fiddle and play with his balls.

They took him to a magistrate,
Who put him in a cell in state,
And left him there to meditate,
And fiddle and play with his balls.

And when they took the case to court,
The lawyer of the lady sought,
To prove that Anthony shouldn't ought,
To fiddle and play with his balls.

The jury said, "It's a bloody disgrace,
Exposing yourself in a public place,
Whacking your tool in a lady's face,

Twisting and playing with your balls."

The judge and jury couldn't agree,
And the judge said, "It's plain to see,
And really and truly I cannot see,
Why a man shouldn't play with his balls."

Then Anthony gave the crowd a shock,
Bold as brass he left the dock,
Swinging his balls around his cock,
Twisting and playing with his balls.

And this is the moral of this song,
If you play with your balls, you can't go wrong,
So bang your cock against the gong,
And fiddle and play with your balls.

11. APPLE TREE

In the shade of the old apple tree, a pair of fine legs I did see,
With some hair at the top, and a little red spot,
It looked like a cherry to me.

In the shade of the old apple tree,
That's were Hilda first showed it to me,
It was hairy and black, and she called it her crack,
It looked like a subway to me.

Well I took out my forty foot pole,
And shoved it right down that dark hole,
I bounced once or twice, it really felt nice,
In the shade of the old apple tree.

As I poked her with my pride of New York,
Which fitted in just like a cork,
I said, "Darlin' don't scream, while I fill you with cream,
In the shade of the old apple tree."

And as we both lay on the grass,
With my two hands around her fat arse,
She said, "If you'll be true, you can have another fuck too,
In the shade of the old apple tree.

12. A - ROVIN'

In Plymouth Town there lived a maid,
Mark well what I do say,
In Plymouth Town there lived a maid,
The mistress of her hoary trade,
I'll go no more a-rovin' with you fair maid.

Chorus:
A-rovin', a-rovin, since fuckin's been my ruin,
I'll go no more a-rovin' with you fair maid.

I put my hand upon her knee, mark well what I do say,
I put my hand upon her knee,
She said "Young man, you're rather free."
I'll go no more a-rovin' with you fair maid.
Chorus
I put my hand upon her thigh, mark well what I do say,
I put my hand upon her thigh,
She said "Young man, you're rather high."
I'll go no more a-rovin' with you fair maid.
Chorus

I put my hand upon her snatch, mark well what I do say,
I put my hand upon her snatch,
She said "Young man, that's my main hatch."
I'll go no more a-rovin' with you fair maid.
Chorus

As I put my hand upon her quim, mark well what I do say,
As I put my hand upon her quim,
She said "For fuck's sake shove it in !"
I'll go no more a-rovin' with you fair maid.
Chorus

She rolled me over on my back, mark well what I do say,
She rolled me over on my back,
And fucked so hard my balls did crack.
I'll go no more a-rovin' with you fair maid.
Chorus

And when she spent my whole year's pay,
Mark well what I do say,
And when she spent my whole year's pay,
She slipped her anchor and sailed away.
I'll go no more a-rovin' with you fair maid.
Chorus

13. AS I WAS WALKING

As I was walking through the woods,
I screwed myself, I knew I would,
I cried for help but no help came
And so I screwed myself again.

As I was walking through St. Paul's
The curate grabbed me by the balls,
I cried for help but no help came
And so he grabbed my balls again.

14. AS OYSTER NAN STOOD BY HER TUB

As Oyster *Nan* stood by her Tub,
To shew her vicious Inclination;
She gave her noblest Parts a Scrub,
And sigh'd for want of Copulation:

A Vintner of no little Fame,
Who excellent Red and White can sell ye,
Beheld the little dirty Dame,
As she stood scratching of her Belly.

Come in, says he, you silly Slut,
'Tis now a rare convenient Minute;
I'll lay the Itching of your Scut,
Except some greedy Devil be in it:

With that the Flat-capt Fusby smil'd,
And would have blush'd, but that she cou'd not;
Alass! says she, we're soon beguil'd,
By Men to do those things we shou'd not.

From Door they went behind the Bar,
As it's by common Fame reported;
And there upon a Turkey Chair,
Unseen the loving Couple sported;

But being call'd by Company,
As he was taking pains to please her;
I'm coming, coming Sir, says he,
My Dear, and so am I, says she, Sir.

Her Mole-hill Belly swell'd about,
Into a Mountain quickly after;
And when the pretty Mouse crept out,
The Creature caus'd a mighty Laughter:

And now she has learnt the pleasing Game,
Altho' much Pain and Shame it cost her;
She daily ventures at the same,
And shuts and opens like an Oyster.

15. BABY FACE
Pubic hair.

You've got the cutest little... pubic hair.
There is no finer anywhere... pubic hair.
Penis or vagina, nothing could be finer.... Pubic hair.
I'm in heaven when I'm in your underwear.
I don't need a shove;

I got a taste of love
From your pretty pubic hair.

16. BAKER'S BOY

The Baker's boy to the Chandlers went,
Some candles for to buy,
But when he got upon the spot, no-one did he es-spy,
So just when he was about to leave,
Thinking that all was dead,
He heard the sound of a rub-a-de-dub right above his head.

Oh, he heard the sound of a rub-a-de-dub
right above his head.

Now the Baker's boy was cunning and wise,
And he crept up those stairs,
And he crept up so silently, he caught them unaware,
And there he saw the Butcher's boy
Between his mistresses' thighs,
And they were having a rub-a-de-dub right before his eyes.

Oh, they were having a rub-a-de-dub right before his eyes.

Oh the Chandler's wife was much alarmed,
And leaping from the bed,
She turned unto the Baker's boy,
And this is what she said,
"If you would but my secret keep, then bear this fact in mind,
You can always come down for a rub-a-de-dub
Whenever you feel inclined"

Oh, you can always come down for a rub-a-de-dub
whenever you feel inclined.

Now the Baker's boy was filled with joy,
At the prospect of such fun,
He vowed he leap on to the bed

When the Butcher's boy was done,
But when he reached those shorter strokes,
How he kissed that Chandler's wife,
For he vowed he'd have a rub-a-de-dub everyday of his life.

Oh, he vowed he'd have a rub-a-de-dub everyday of his life.

Now in the morn when he awoke, all over he did ache,
His back was sore, his balls were raw, all over he did shake,
But when he looked at his John Tom,
He saw he'd done the trick,
For the consequences of his rub-a-de-dub
Was pimples on his prick.

Oh, the consequences of his rub-a-de-dub was pimples on
his prick.

The Chandler returned and entered the shop,
And quickly smelt a rat,
Seeing his wife all naked there, her hand upon her twat,
The Chandler's wife ran from the room,
Expecting the boy had fled,
But he was having a rub-a-de-dub all by himself in bed.

Oh, he was having a rub-a-de-dub all by himself in bed.

Now the Baker's boy to the doctor's went
Some ointment for to buy,
The doctor looked him up and down,
And heaved a mighty sigh,
"My boy, my boy," the doctor said,
"You've been a bloody fool,
For the consequence of your rub-a-de-dub
Is I've got to cut off your tool !"

Oh, the consequence of your rub-a-de-dub is I've got to cut
off your tool !

The moral of this story is, I'm sure that you should know,

Enthusiastic amateurs are worse than any pro,
And if you would a wooing go, and self control you lack,
Whenever you have a rub-a-de-dub, be sure to wear a mack.

Oh, whenever you have a rub-a-de-dub,
be sure to wear a mack.

17. BALLS OF KERRYMUIR

Four & twenty virgins came down from Inverness,
And when the ball was over there was four and twenty less.

 Chorus ;   Balls to your partner, arse against the wall,
 If you never get Fucked on a saturday night,
 You'll never get Fucked at all.

The village postman he was there, he had a dose of pox,
He couldn't fuck the women so he Fucked the letterbox.
 Chorus

The village plumber he was there, he felt a fucking fool,
He walked eleven miles or more and forgot to bring his tool.
 Chorus

There was fucking in the hallways and fucking in the ricks,
You couldn't hear the music for the swishing of the pricks.
 Chorus

There was fucking in the ante-room and fucking on the
stairs,
You couldn't see the carpet for the short and curly hairs.
 Chorus

The parson's daughter she was there, the cunning little runt,
With poison ivy up her arse, and a thistle up her cunt.
 Chorus

The vicar's wife she was there, sitting by the fire,
Knitting rubber johnies from an indian rubber tyre.

Chorus

The village idiot he was there, sitting up a pole,
He pulled his foreskin over his head and whistled down the hole.
 Chorus

The village Smithy he was there, sitting by the fire,
Doing abortions by the score with a piece of red hot wire.
 Chorus

The Smithy's brother he was there, a mighty man was he,
He lined them up against the wall and fucked them three by three.
 Chorus

Giles he played a dirty trick, we cannot let it pass,
He showed a lass his mighty prick and shoved it up her arse.
 Chorus

Jock McTavish he was there, his prick was long and broad,
When he Fucked the farmers wife she had to be rebored.
 Chorus

Little Tommy he was there, he was only eight,
He couldn't fuck the women so he had to masterbate.
 Chorus

And when the ball was over, everyone confessed,
They all enjoyed the dancing, but the fucking was the best.

18. BALLS TO YOUR PARTNER
(The Ball Of Kerrymuir)

CHORUS:Balls to your partner,
Ass against the wall,
If you've never been laid on Saturday night,
You've never been laid at all.

Four and twenty virgins, Came down from Inverness,
And when the ball was over, There were four and twenty
less.

Four and twenty whores, Came up from Glockamore,
And when the ball was over, They were all of them double
bore.

The village plumber he was there, He felt an awful fool,
He'd come eleven leagues or more, And forgot to bring his
tool.

There was fucking in the hallways, And fucking in the ricks,
You couldn't hear the music For the swishing of the pricks.

They were fucking in the Barley. They were fucking in the
oats.
Some were fucking sheep, but most were fucking goats.

There was fucking in the kitchen, And fucking in the halls,
You couldn't hear the music for The clanging of the balls.

There was fucking in the parlor, And fucking on the stairs,
You couldn't see the carpet For the mass of public hairs.

I put my head upon her lap, and she put hers in mine.
We sucked a bit and blowed a bit and that's called sixty-
nine.

The parson's daughter she was there, The cunning little
runt,
With poison ivy up her ass, And thistle up her cunt.

The village whore she was there, Doing a really good stunt
Stuck to the ceiling By the suction of her cunt.

The village idiot he was there Sitting on a pole

Pulled his foreskin over his head, And whistled though the hole.

The mayors wife she was there Lying on the floor
Every time she spread he legs The suction closed the door

Grandma and Grandpa they were there Sitting by the fire
Knitting prophylactics Out of old rubber tires.

The village postman he was there He had a case of the pox
Couldn't fuck the women, So he fucked a letter box.

Little Tommy he was there, He was only eight
Couldn't fuck the women So he had to masturbate.

The blacksmith's brother he was there A mighty stud was he
Lined 'em up against the wall, And fucked 'em three-by-three.

The village hooker she was there Feeling mighty fine
Lined 'em up against the wall And fucked 'em nine-by-nine.

The village rugger he was there the mightiest of men
Lined 'em up against the wall And fucked em ten-by-ten.

The village magician he was there Up to his favorite trick
Pulling his asshole over his head And standing on his prick.

Father O'Flanagan he was there And in the corner sat
Amusing himself by abusing himself And catching it in his hat.

Dino had an even stroke His skill was much admired
He gratified one cunt at a time Until his skill expired.

Jock McVennig he was there A looking for a fuck
But every cunt was occupied And he was out of luck.

Michael Lee when he got the there His prick was long and high
But when he fucked her forty times He was fucking mighty dry.

McTavish, oh yes, he was there His prick was long and broad
And when he fucked the furriers wife She had to be rebored.

The village dogcatcher Proved he was no slouch
Went out and caught the neighbors dog And fucked it on the couch.

The village gynecologist he was there On a beaver hunt
Pulled down all the women's pants And probed through all their cunts.

The village dunce he was there All alone he stands
Amusing himself by abusing himself And using both his hands.

The village idiot he was there, Up to this and that,
Amusing himself by abusing himself, And catching it in his hat.

The bride was in the kitchen Explaining to the groom,
The vagina not the rectum Is the entrance to the womb.

The village magician he was there, Up to his favorite trick,
Pulling his foreskin over his head, And disappearing up his prick.

The village giant he was there, A mighty man was he,
He lined them up against the wall And fucked them three by three.

The vicar and his wife were there, Having lots of fun,
The parson had his finger Up another lady's bun.

The village doctor he was there, He had his bag of tricks,
And in between the dances He was sterilizing pricks.

Father O'Flanagan he was there, And in the corner he sat,
Amusing himself by abusing himself And catching it in his had.

There was fucking on the couches, There was fucking on the cots,
And lying up against the wall Were rows of grinning twats.

Giles he played a dirty trick, We cannot let it pass,
He showed a lass his mighty prick Then shoved it up her ass.

Mrs. O'Maley she was there, She had the crowd in fits,
A jumping off the mantelpiece And bouncing off her tits.

Jackie Stewart did his fucking, Right upon the moor,
It was, he thought, much better Than fucking on the floor.

Jock McDougall he was there, A looking for a fuck,
But every quim was occupied And he was out of luck.

The huntsman's daughter she was there, Tired from the hunt,
A wreath of roses around her ass And a carrot up her cunt.

The chimney sweep he was there, They had to throw him out,
For every time he passed some wind The room was filled with soot.

The village economist he was there, His prick held in his hand,
Waiting for the moment when Supply would meet demand.

The village blacksmith he was there, Sitting by the fire,
Doing abortions by the score With a piece of red hot wire.

The village postman he was there, The poor man had the pox,
He couldn't fuck the lasses So he fucked the letter box.

The blacksmith's father he was there, A roaring like a lion,
He'd cut his cock off in the forge So he used his rod of iron.

Dino had an even stroke, His skill was much admired,
He fucked away half the night Until his cock expired.

The village butcher he was there, Cleaver in his hand,
Every time he turned around He circumcised the band.

The village virgin she was there, All dressed in frilly pink,
She took the boys behind the fence And made their fingers stink.

Willy Roberts he arrived, His prick was all alert,
But when the night was done "Twas dangling in the dirt."

Now little Willy he was there, But he was only eight,
He couldn't catch a harlot So he had to masturbate.

The village veteran he was there, His balls were made of brass,
And when he blew a fart, my lads, The sparks flew out his ass.

Little Jimmy he was there, The leader of the choir,
He hit the balls of all the boys To make their voices higher.

The village leper he was there, Sitting on a log,
Peeling foreskin off his cock And feeding it to his dog.

Another blacksmith he was there, Tending to his fires,
Making prophylactics Out of motorcycle tires.

The village builder he was there, He brought his bag of tricks,
He poured cement in all the holes And blunted all the pricks.

The village cripple he was there, He wasn't very much,
Took the girls behind the house And fucked them with his crutch.

Wee MacGregor he was there, His pint of beer he'd split,
It mingled with the semen That was trickling down his kilt.

The mayor's daughter she was there, She had the crowd in fits,
Sliding down the banister And bouncing on her tits.

The village stable boy he was there, The bastard was quite coarse,
We caught him in the stable With his cock inside a horse.

The village parson he was there, All dressed up in his shroud,
Swinging on the chandelier Pissing on the crowd.

And when the ball was over, What a sight to see,
Four and twenty maidenheads A hanging from a tree.

And when the ball was over, Everyone did confess,
They all enjoyed the dancing But the FUCKING was the best.

Mrs. O'Leary she was there, Swingin' from the chandelier,
Spilling her menstrual juices Into everybody's beer.

The village cook he was there, The bastard was quite crude,
They caught him in the kitchen Masturbating in the food.

The Jersey girl was standin' there, Her but against the wall,
"Put your money on the table boys, I'm goin' to do youse all!"

The parson's wife she was there, And she was worst of all,
Pulled her skirt above her head And shouted, "FUCK IT
ALL."

The vicar's wife she was there, Sitting by the fire,
Knitting contraceptives Out of india rubber tires.

Sergeant Murphy he was there, The pride of the Force,
They caught him behind the barn Jacking off a horse.

And when the ball was over, All the guests confessed,
The music was the finest But the FUCKING was the best.

And so the ball was over, All went home to rest,
The music had been exquisite Still the FUCKING was the
best.

And finally there was the Johnnie Rugger He seemed like
quite a stud.
But when it came to fucking His pecker was a dud.

19. BANG BANG LULU

Chorus :
Bang Bang Lulu, Lulu's gone away,
Who are we gonna bang bang, when Lulu's gone away,

I took her to the pictures, we sat down in the stalls,
Every time the lights went out, she grabbed me by the .....
Chorus

She and I went fishing in a dainty little punt,
Every time I hooked a sprat, she stuffed it up her .....
Chorus

Lulu's got a rooster, Lulu's got a duck,
She put them in a bathtub to see if they would .....
Chorus

Lulu had a boyfriend, his name was Michael Hunt,
She used to like him very much, 'cos he kissed her on the
.....
Chorus

Lulu had a baby, it was an awful shock,
She couldn't call it Lulu, 'cos the bastard had a .....
Chorus

Lulu had a bicycle, the seat was very blunt,
Every time she pedalled hard, it sunk into her .....
Chorus

I wish I was her chamber pot, 'twould be the height of bliss,
I'd see her lovely maidenhead, each time she took a .....
Chorus

20 BARNACLE BILL THE SAILOR

(Sung to the tune of "Barnacle Bill the Sailor")

WOMAN'S VOICE:
Who's that knocking at my door? Who's that knocking at my
door?
Who's that knocking at my door? Cried the fair young
maiden.

MAN'S VOICE:
Oh, it's only me from across the sea.
Cried Barnacle Bill the Sailor.

WOMAN'S VOICE:
Why are you knocking at my door?
Why are you knocking at my door?
Why are you knocking at my door?
Cried the fair young maiden.

MAN'S VOICE:
'Cos I'm young enough, and ready and tough.

Cried Barnacle Bill the Sailor.

Will you take me to the dance?
To hell with the dance down with your pants.

You can sleep upon the floor.
I'll not sleep on the floor you dirty whore.

You can sleep upon the mat.
Oh, bugger the mat you can't fuck that.

You can sleep upon the stairs.
Oh, fuck the stairs they haven't got hairs.

What's that running up my blouse?
It's only me mitt to grab yer tit.

You can sleep between my tits.
Oh, bugger your tits they give me the shits.
You can sleep between my thighs.
Bugger your thighs they're covered in flies.

You can sleep within my cunt.
Oh, bugger your cunt but I'll fuck for a stunt.

What's that running in and out?
It's only me cock, it's as hard as a rock.

What's that running down my leg?
It's only me shot that missed yer twat.

What if my parents should find out?
We'll eat your ma and blow your pa.

What if my mother should disagree?
If yer ma'll agree we'll make it three.

What if we should get VD?
We'll pick the sores and fuck some more.

What if we should get the (clap!)?
Gotta be willin' to take penicillin.

What if I should have a child?
We'll drown the bugger and fuck for another.

What if we should have a girl?
We'll dig a ditch and bury the bitch.

What if we should have a boy?
He'll play rugby and fuck like me.

What'll we do when the baby's born
We'll drown the bugger and fuck for another.

What if you should go to jail?
I'll pick the lock with my ten-foot cock.

What if we should go to prison?
I'll swing my balls and knock down the walls.

21. BASTARD KING OF ENGLAND

Oh, the minstrels sing of an English King,
Who lived long years ago,
Who ruled his land with an iron hand,
But his mind was weak and low.
He used to hunt the royal stag, within the royal wood,
But better than this he loved the bliss of pulling his royal
pud.

Chorus :
He was dirty and lousy and covered in fleas,
His terrible tool hung down to his knees,
God save the bastard King of England.

The Queen of Spain was an amorous dame,
And a silly old witch was she,

For she longed to fool with his majesty's tool,
So far across the sea.
So she sent a royal message, with a royal messenger,
Inviting the king to bring his ding,
And spend the week with her.
Chorus

When news of this reached Philip of France,
He swore before his court,
"The Queen prefers my rival because my dork is short."
So he sent the Duke of Zippety-Zap,
To slip the Queen a dose of clap,
To pass it on to the bastard King of England.
Chorus

When news of this foul dastardly deed,
Reached fair Windsor Hall,
The king swore by the royal whore,
He'd have the Frenchman's balls.
So he offered half his kingdom,
And the contents of the Queen's pants,
To any loyal subject who would nut the king of France.
Chorus

So the noble Duke of Middlesex, he took himself to France,
He swore he was a fairy, so the king took down his pants.
On Philip's dong he tied a thong,
Leaped on his horse and galloped along,
Dragging the Frenchman back to merry England.
Chorus

Now the king threw up his breakfast,
and shat all over the floor,
For during the ride, the Frenchman's pride
Has stretched a yard or more.
And all the whores in their silken drawers,
Came down to London town,
And shouted around the battlements,
"To hell with the British crown !"

Chorus

Rule Britannia, marmalade and jam, five Chinese crackers
up yer arsehole   Bang, Bang, Bang, Bang, BANG.

22. BE KIND TO YOUR WEB-FOOTED FRIENDS

(Sung to the tune of "Stars and Stripes Forever")

Be kind to your web-footed friends
For a duck may be somebody's mother
Be kind to your friends in the swamp
Where the weather is cool and damp
Now you may think that this is the end
Well it is ...

23. BESTIALITY'S BEST

(Sung to the tune of "Wallaby Song")

CHORUS:Bestiality's best boys, bestiality's best.
Fuck a wallaby!
Bestiality's best boys, bestiality's best.
Fuck a wallaby!

Blow your rocks in an ox boys, blow your rocks in an ox.
Fuck a wallaby!
Blow your rocks in an ox boys, blow your rocks in an ox.
Fuck a wallaby!

In the spunk of a skunk boys, in the spunk of a skunk.
Fuck a wallaby!
In the spunk of a skunk boys, in the spunk of a skunk.
Fuck a wallaby!

In the rear of a deer boys, in the rear of a deer.
Fuck a wallaby!
In the rear of a deer boys, in the rear of a deer.
Fuck a wallaby!

24. BILL BAILEY

(Sung to the tune of "Bill Bailey")

CHORUS: Rip roar a tie-tie-ay,
Rip roar a tie-tie-ay, Rip roar a tie-tie.
Rip roar a tucky-tucky, Rip roar a tucky-tucky-aaaay.

I saw Bill Bailey, out with the ladies
Under a starry sky
Then along came his wife
With a bloody great knife
And she chopped off the end
Of his tooral-ly-ay, Hey!

Off to the courthouse, he was lumbered
Charged with adultery
But the charge wouldn't stick
For he hadn't a prick
Cause she chopped off the end
Of his tooral-ly-ay, Hey!

25. BLACK BULL

The big black bull came down from the mountain,
Houston Sam Houston,
The big black bull came down from the mountain
Long time ago
            Chorus ;
 It was a long time ago - o - o,
 A long time ago - o - o,
_(repeat first line of verse)
 Long time ago.

He spied a heifer in the pasture,
Houston Sam Houston,
He spied a heifer in the pasture, long time ago.
 Chorus

There was a fence around that pasture,
Houston Sam Houston,
There was a fence around that pasture, long time ago.
Chorus

He jumped that fence and he `Oofed' that heifer,
Houston Sam Houston,
He jumped that fence and he `Oofed' that heifer,
Long time ago.
 Chorus

He missed his mark and he `Fffd' on the pasture,
Houston Sam Houston,
He missed his mark and he `Fffd' on the pasture,
Long time ago.
 Chorus
The big black bull returned to the mountain,
Houston Sam Houston,
The big black bull returned to the mountain, long time ago.
 Chorus

His head hung low but his balls hung lower,
Houston Sam Houston,
His head hung low but his balls hung lower, long time ago.
 Chorus

26. BLACK VELVET BAND

(Sung to the tune of "Black Velvet Band")

CHORUS: Her eyes they shone like the diamond,
They call her the Queen of the land.
And her hair hung over her shoulders,
Tied up with a black velvet band.

In a neat little town they call Belfast,
Apprentice to trade I was found,
Many an hour sweet happiness,
Have I spent in this neat little town,
Till bad misfortune befell me,

Which caused me to stray from the land,
Far away from my friends and relations,
Betrayed by the black velvet band.

Well I was out strolling one evening,
Not meaning to go very far
When I met with a pretty young damsel
She was selling her trade in a bar
She was both fair and handsome,
And her neck it was just like a swan,
And her hair it hung it over her shoulder,
Tied up with a black velvet band.

I took a stroll with this pretty fair maid,
And the gentleman passing us by,
Well I knew she meant the doing of him,
By the look in her roguish black-eye,
The gold watch she took from his pocket,
And placed it right into my hand,
On the very first day that I met her,
Bad luck from the black velvet band.

Next morning before judge and jury
For our trial I had to appear
The judge, he said, "Young fellow
The case against you is quite clear
And seven years is your sentence
You're going to Van Dieman's Land
Far away from your friends and relations
Betrayed by the black velvet band.

So come all you jolly young fellows
I'd have you take warning by me
And whenever you're out on the liquor
Beware of the pretty colleen
They'll fill your with whiskey and porter
Until you're not able to stand
And the very next thing that you know
You're landed in Van Dieman's Land.

27. BLINDED BY TURDS

There was an old lady who lived in our town,
Whose arsehole was stuffed with the great smelly brown,
She took a large dose without reading the box,
Before she could strip, turds were flying like rocks.

Chorus:
Singing Too-ra-la, oo-ra-la, oo-ra-la ay,
Too-ra-la, oo-ra-la, oo-ra-la ay,
(last 2 lines of verse)

She ran to the window and stuck out her arse,
Just as a night watchman happened to pass,
He smelled a strong fart settling down on that place,
When a fucking big turd hit him straight in the face.
Chorus

He ran to the east and he ran to the west,
When a fast flying turd landed right on his chest,
He ran to the north and he ran to the south,
When a huge dark brown turd hit him right in the mouth.
Chorus

So next time you walk out be careful of shit,
Look out where you walk and don't step in it,
And pity the watchman whose sign bears these words,
"I am an old man who was blinded by turds."
Chorus

And as you pass by, please do not spit,
On the sorrowful fellow who's blinded by shit.

28. BLOWZABELLA MY BOUNCING DOXIE

He. **Blowzabella** my bouncing Doxie,
Come let's trudge it to **Kirkham** Fair,
There's stout Liquor enough to Fox me,
And young Cullies to buy thy Ware.

She. Mind your Matters ye Sot without medling
How I manage the sale of my Toys,
Get by Piping as I do by Pedling,
You need never want me for supplies.

He. God-a-mercy my Sweeting, I find thou think'st fitting,
To hint by this twitting, I owe thee a Crown;

She. Tho' for that I've been staying, a greater Debt's paying,
Your rate of delaying will never Compound.

He. I'll come home when my Pouch is full,
And soundly pay thee all old Arrears;

She. You'll forget it your Pate's so dull,
As by drowzy Neglect appears.

He. May the Drone of my Bag never hum,
If I fail to remember my *Blowse*;

She. May my Buttocks be ev'ry ones Drum,
If I think thou wilt pay me a Souse.

He. Squeakham, Squeakham, Bag-pipe will make 'em,
Whisking, Frisking, Money brings in,
She. Smoaking, Toping, Landlady groping,
Whores and Scores will spend it again.

He. By the best as I guess in the Town,
I swear thou shalt have e'ery Groat;

She. By the worst that a Woman e'er found,
If I have it will signify nought;

He. If good Nature works no better,
Blowzabella I'd have you to know,
Though you fancy my Stock is so low,
I've more Rhino than always I show,
For some good Reasons of State that I know.

She. Since your Cheating I always knew,
For my Ware I got something too,
I've more Sence than to tell to you.

He. Singly then let's imploy Wit,
I'll use Pipe as my gain does hit,

She. And If I a new Chapman get,
You'll be easy too,

He. Easy as any worn out Shoo.

[CHORUS of both.]
Free and Frolick we'll Couple Gratis
Thus we'll show all the Human Race;
That the best of the Marriage State is,
Blowzabella's *and* Collin's *Case.*

29. BOY MEETS GIRL

Boy meets girl, holds her hand,
Visions of a promised land,
Tender words, cling and kiss,
Crafty feel, heavenly bliss,
Nibble nipples, squeeze thighs,
Gets a beat, feels a rise,
Eyes ablaze, drawers down,
Really starts to go to town,
Legs outspread, virgin lass,
Fanny foams like bottled Bass,
Ram it home, moans of joy,
Teenage love, girl meets boy,
Love's a jewel, pearls he's won,

Shoots his load, what's he done,
Comes the pay off, here's the rub,
He's got her in the pudding club,
Comes the wedding, bridesmaids flap,
Love and cherish, all that crap,
A tubby tum, weighty gain,
Prams and nappies, labour pain,
Begins to realize what he did,
Nagging wife and screaming kid,
Sweats his prick off, works his stint;
Only pleasure is evening time,
When mattress creaks she's off again,
Can't forsake those sexy habits,
Breeding kids like bloody rabbits.

30 BROTHER JOHNNY

("Johnny" is replaced by the name of the person who
messes up a solo.)

Here's to Brother Johnny, Brother Johnny, Brother Johnny.
Here's to Brother Johnny who's with us tonight.
He beats it, he eats it, he often mistreats it.
Here's to Brother Johnny who's with us tonight.

31. BY THE LIGHT

(Sung to the tune of "By The Light Of The Silvery Moon")

By the light,
tish, tish, tish, tish, tish, tish,
Of the flickering match,
tish, tish, tish, tish, tish, tish,
I saw her snatch,
tish, tish, tish, tish, tish, tish,
In the watermelon patch,
tish, tish, tish, tish, tish, tish.
By the light,
tish, tish, tish, tish, tish, tish,
Of the flickering match,

tish, tish, tish, tish, tish, tish,
I saw her gleam, I heard her scream,
you are burning my snatch,
tish, tish, tish, tish, tish, tish,
With your God damned match,
tish, tish, tish, tish, tish, tish.

32. BYE, BYE, BLACKBIRD

(Sung to the tune of "Bye, Bye, Blackbird")

Once a boy was no good,
Took a girl into a wood,
Bye, Bye, Blackbird.

Laid her down upon the grass,
Pinched her tits and slapped her ass,
Blackbird Bye, Bye,.

Took her where nobody else could find her,
To a place where he could really grind her,
Bye, Bye, Blackbird.

Rolled her over on her front,
Shoved his prick right up her cunt,
Blackbird Bye, Bye,.

But this girl was no sport,
Took her story to a court,
Bye, Bye, Blackbird.

Told her story in the morn,
All the jury had a horn,
Blackbird, Bye, Bye.

Then the judge came to his decision,
This poor sod got eighteen months in prison,
Bye, Bye, Blackbird.

So next time, boy, do it right,

Stuff her cunt with dynamite,
Blackbird, Bye, Bye.

33. CALIFORNIA DRINKING SONG

Oh, we had a little party down in Newport,
There was Harry, there was Mary, there was Grace.
Oh, we had a little party down in Newport,
And we had to carry Harry from the place.

Oh, we had to carry Harry to the ferry,
And we had to carry him to the shore.
And the reason that we had to carry Harry to the ferry,
Was that Harry couldn't carry anymore.

For California, for California,
The hills resound the cry, we're out to do or die.
For California, for California,
We'll win the game or know the reason why.

And when the game is over we will buy a case of booze,
And we'll drink to California 'til we wallow in our shoes.
So drink, tra-la-la
Drink, drank, drunk last night
Drunk the night before
Gonna get drunk tonight like we've never been drunk before
'Cause when I'm drunk I'm as happy as can be
For I'm a member of the Souse family.
Oh, the Souse family is the best family
That ever came over from old Germany.
There's the Highland Dutch and the Lowland Dutch,
And the goddamn Dutch and the Irish.

Sing Glorious! Victorious!
One keg of beer for the four of us.
Sing Glory be to God that there are no more of us,
For one of us could drink it all alone, damned near.

Here's to the Irish. Dead drunk!

The lucky stiffs.
They had four fifths,
And a six pack, too. Brew 102.
The lucky stiffs

34. CAN YOU WALK A LITTLE WAY WITH IT IN?

(Sung to the tune of "She'll Be Coming Round The Mountain")

Can you walk a little way with it in, with it in?
Can you walk a little way with it in?
"Oh," she answered with a smile,
"I can walk a fucking mile,
With it in, with it in, with it in."

35. CAROLINA

Way down in Alabama where the bullshit runs thick,
The girls are so pretty the babies come quick,
There lives Carolina, the girl I adore,
My hot fucking, cock sucking Mexican whore.

She's handy, she's bandy, she shags in the street,
Whenever you meet her, she's always on heat,
If you leave your flies open, she's after your meat,
And the smell of her cunt knocks you right off your feet.

One night I was riding down by the falls,
One hand on my pistol, the other on my balls,
I saw Carolina using a stick,
Instead of the end of a cow-puncher's prick.

I caressed her, undressed her and laid her down there,
And parted the tresses of curly brown hair,
Inserted the prick of my sturdy horse,
And then there began a strange intercourse.

Faster & faster went my sturdy steed,
Until Carolina rejoiced at the speed,
When all of a sudden my horse did back fire,
And shot Carolina right into the mire.

Up got Carolina all covered in muck,
And said, "Oh my dear, what a glorious fuck."
Took two paces forward, fell flat on the floor,
And that was the end of the cow-puncher's whore.

36. CASEY JONES

Casey Jones was a son of a bitch,
Drove a steam engine through a forty foot ditch,
Pissed on the whistle and shit on bell,
And he went through Chicago like a bat out of hell.

Chorus:
Casey Jones, mounted to his cabin,
Casey Jones, had his pecker in his hand,
Casey Jones, mounted to his cabin,
"Bend over ladies, I'm a railroad man."

It happened one morning about a quarter to four,
Pulled up in front of a whorehouse door,
Climbed through the window with his cock in his hand,
Said, "I'll prove I'm a railroad man."
Chorus

He lined a hundred whores up against the wall,
And he bet ten dollars he could fuck 'em all,
He fucked ninety eight and his balls turned blue,
He took a shot of whisky and fucked the other two.
Chorus

Casey Jones was a son of a bitch,
His balls were covered with the whorehouse itch,
He left that house with his pecker in his hand,
Says to the whores, "I'm a railroad man."

Chorus

Casey Jones said before he died,
There were five more things he would like to ride,
Bicycle, tricycle, automobile,
A bow legged nigger and a ferris wheel.
Chorus

They were rolling down the line about half past two,
Casey pissed in the fire and the boiler blew,
That was the end of Casey Jones's reign,
As the stinking fucker who drove a train.
Chorus

37. CATHUSALEM

CHORUS:Hi ho Cathusalem, Cathusalem, Cathusalem,
Hi ho Cathusalem, Harlot of Jerusalem.
In the days of old there lived a maid,
She was the Mistress of her trade,
A prostitute of high repute,
The harlot of Jerusalem.

Though she screwed for many a year,
Of pregnancy she had no fear,
She washed her passage with beer,
The best in all Jerusalem.

Now in a hovel by the wall,
A student lived with but one ball,
Who'd been through all, or nearly all,
The harlots of Jerusalem.

His phallic limb was lean and tall,
His phallic art caused all to fall,
And victims lined the Wailing Wall,
That goes around Jerusalem.

One night returning from a spree,

With customary whore-lust he,
Made up his mind to call and see,
The harlot of Jerusalem.

It was for her no fortune good,
That he needed to root his pud,
And chose her out of all the breed,
Of harlots of Jerusalem.

With artful eye and leering look
He took out from its filthy-nook,
His organ stisted like a crook,
The Pride of Old Jerusalem.

He put the whore against the slum,
And tied her at the knee and bum,
Just where the strain would come,
Upon the fair Cathusalem.

He seized the harlot by the bun,
And rattling like a Lewis gun,
He sewed the seed of many a son,
Into the fair Cathusalem.

Then up there came an Onanite,
With warty balls smeared with shit,
He'd sworn he would ball that night,
The harlot of Jerusalem.

So when he saw the grunting pair,
With roars of rage he rent the air,
Vowed that he would soon take care,
Of the harlot of Jerusalem.

He seized the bastard by his crook,
And with a single look,
Flung him over Kedren's Brook,
That babbles past Jerusalem.

The student gave a furious roar,
And rushed to even up the score,
And with his swollen cock did bore,
The rapist of Cathusalem.

And reeling full of rags and fight,
He pushed the bastard Onanite,
And rubbed his face in Cathy's shit,
The foulest in Jerusalem.

Cathusalem she knew her part,
She closed her ass and blew a fart,
That sent him flying like a dart,
Right over old Jerusalem.

And buzzing like a bumble bee,
He flew straight out towards the sea,
But caught his asshole in a tree,
That grows in old Jerusalem.

And to this day you still can see,
His asshole hanging from that tree,
Let that to you a warning be,
When passing through Jerusalem.

And when the moon is bright and red,
A castrated fern sails overhead,
Still raining curses on the head,
Of the harlot of Jerusalem.

It was a sight to make you sick,
To hear him grunt so fast & quick,
As he tore with his crooked dick,
The womb of fair Cathusalem.

As for the student and his lass,
Many a playful night did pass,
Until she joined the V.D. class,
For harlots of Jerusalem.

38. CATS ON THE ROOFTOP

CHORUS:Singing cats on the rooftop, cats on the tiles,
Cats with the clap and cats with the piles,
Cats with their asses wreathed in smiles,
As they revel in the joys of fornication.

When you wake up in the morn with the devil of a stand,
From the pressure of the liquid on the seminary gland,
If you haven't got a woman use you own horny hand,
As you revel in the joys of masturbation.

The Regimental Sergeant Major leads a miserable life,
He can't afford a mistress and he doesn't have a wife,
So he puts it up the bottom of the Regimental Fife,
As he revels in the joys of fornication.

When you find yourself in springtime with a surge of sexual
joy,
And your wife has got the rag on and your daughter's rather
coy,
Then jam it up the arse hole of your favorite choirboy,
As you revel in a smooth ejaculation.

The ostrich on the pampas is a solitary chick,
Without the opportunity to dip its wick,
But whenever it does it slips in thick,
As he revels in the joys of fornication.

The elephant's dong is big and round,
A small one weighs a thousand pound,
Two together shake the ground,
As they revel in the joys of fornication.

The oyster is a paragon of purity,
And you can't tell the he from the she,
But he can tell and so can she,
As they revel in the joys of fornication.

The donkey is a lonely bloke,
He hardly ever gets a poke,
But when he does he lets it soak,
As he revels in the joys of fornication.

The hippopotamus so it seems,
Rarely, if ever, has wet dreams,
But when he does he comes in streams,
As he revels in the joys of fornication.

The camel likes to have his fun,
His night is made when he is done,
He always gets two humps for one,
As he revels in the joys of fornication.

The flea cavorts among the trees,
And there consorts with whom he please,
To fill the land with bastard fleas,
As he revels in the joys of fornication.

The ape is small and rather slow,
Erect he stands a foot or so,
So when he comes it's time to go,
As he revels in the joys of fornication.

The orangutan is a colorful sight,
There's a glow on its arse likke a pilot light,
As it jumps and it leaps in the night,
As he revels in the joys of fornication.

Long-legged curates grind like goats,
Pale-faced spinsters shag like stoats,
And the whole damn works stands by and gloats,
As they revel in the joys of fornication.

A thousand verses all in rhyme,
To sit and sing them seems a crime,
When we could better spend our time,
Revelling in the joys of fornication.

39. CHARLOTTE THE HARLOT

(Sung to the tune of "Sweet Betsy From Pike")

CHORUS:She's filthy, she's nasty,
    She spits on the floor,
Charlotte the Harlot, the cowpuncher's whore.

Way out in the wild west where the bullshit lies thick,
Where the women are women and the cowboys come quick,
There lives a fair maiden of forty or more,
Charlotte the Harlot, the cowpuncher's whore.

She's handy, she's bandy, she screws in the street,
Whenever you meet her she's always in heat,
If you leave your fly open she's after your meat,
And the small of her cunt knocks you right off your feet.

She's easy, she's breezy, she's my hearts delight,
I'll fuck her by day and fuck her by night,
And each time I fuck her she shouts out, "Encore,"
I call that great fucking and I want some more.

One night on the prairie while riding along,
One hand on my pistol and one on my dong,
What should I spy but the maid I adore,
Charlotte the Harlot, the cowpuncher's whore.

One night I was riding way down by the falls,
One hand on my pistol, the other on my balls,
What should I see but Charlotte using a stick,
Instead of the end of a cowpuncher's prick.

One night on the desert her legs opened wide,
A rattlesnake saw it and climbed up inside,
Now all the cowboys on Saturday night,
Come see the vagina that rattles and bites.

I leapt from my saddle and reached for her crack,
But the damn thing was rattling and bit me back,

I pulled out my six gun and aimed for its head,
But the damn thing misfired and shot Charlotte instead.

I caressed her, undressed her, and laid her down there,
And parted the tresses of curly brown hair,
Inserted the penis of my sturdy horse,
And then there began a strange intercourse.

Faster and faster went my sturdy steed,
Until Charlotte rejoiced at the speed,
When all of a sudden my horse did backfire,
And shot Charlotte right into the mire.

He got Charlotte all covered in muck,
And said, "Oh dear, cowboy, what a glorious fuck,"
She stepped a pace forward and fell flat on the floor,
And that was the end of the cowpuncher's whore.

The funeral procession was forty miles long,
And all of the cowboys were singing the song,
"Here lies a maiden who never kept score,
Charlotte the Harlot, the cowpuncher's whore."

40. CHARLOTTE THE HARLOT LAY DYING

CHORUS:"I've been had by the army, the navy,
By a bullfighting toreador,
By dages and dronges and dinges,
But never by maggots before,
So roll back your dirty old assholes,
And give me the cream of your nuts."
So they rolled back their dirty old assholes,
And played "Home Sweet Home" on her guts.

Charlotte the Harlot lay dying,
A piss-pot supported her head,
The blow-flies were buzzing around her,

She lay on her left tit and said:

Charlotte the Harlot repented,
She'd never have another bang,
She wanted to go to heaven,
So she rolled on her right tit and sang:

Charlotte the Harlot was buried,
The town was much quieter than before,
But one night at the local brothel,
Her ghost appeared in the beer.

41. CHRISTOPHER COLUMBO

CHORUS:His balls they were so round - o
His cock hung to the ground - o
That fornicating, copulating
Son-of-a-bitch Columbo.
In fourteen hundred and ninety-two
A man whose name was Chris
Stood by the Trevi fountain
Indulging in a piss.

Along did come the Queen of Spain
And glimpsing there his dong,
Forthwith was smitten with desire
And knew not right from wrong.

"Oh, Isabelle," Columbo said,
A-waving of his balls,
"The world is round as these are,
I feel that duty calls."

"Just wait a bit," said Isabelle,
"And don't forget essentials,
For I've a mind to have a grind
And check on your credentials."

She gave her guest no time for rest,

The pace was fairly killing,
With legs apart he gave the tart
A cream and cherry filling.

With lustful shout they ran about
And practiced copulation,
And when they left to sail away
They'd doubled the population.

And when his men pulled out again,
And reckoned all their score up,
They'd caught a pox from every box
That syphilized all Europe.

Three ships set sail that sunny day,
They all were triple deckers,
The queen she waived her handkerchief
Columbo waived his pecker.

For forty days and forty nights
He sailed the broad Atlantic,
Columbo and his scurvy crew
For want of a screw were frantic.

The cabin boy, the cabin boy,
That dirty little nipper,
He packed his ass with broken glass
And circumcised his skipper.

The first mate's name was John,
They loved him like a brother,
And every night in the pale moonlight
They corn-holed each other.

The third mate's name was Higgins,
And Higgins had a big 'un,
Twice round his neck, twice round the deck,
The rest was used for riggin.

The cook, that rotten man,
He was a dirty demon,
He served the crew a menstrual stew,
And flavored it with semen.

An Indian maid ran down the beach,
Columbo he pursued her,
The white of an egg ran down her leg,
Columbo he unscrewed her.

And when they got to Yankee land,
The spied a Yankee harlot,
When they came her arse was lily-white,
When they left her arse was scarlet.

42 CHRISTOPHER ROBIN
(Sung to the tune of "Christopher Robin")

Little boy kneels at the foot of the stairs
Clutched in his hand are a bunch of white hairs
Oh my just fancy that
Christopher Robin castrated the cat.

Little boy kneels at the foot of the bed
Lily-white hands are caressing his head
Oh my couldn't be worse
Christopher Robin is shagging his nurse.

Little boy sits on the lavatory pan
Gently caressing his little old man
Flip flop into the tank
Christopher Robin is having a wank.

43. CLEMENTINE
(Sung to the tune of "Clementine")

CHORUS: I owe my darlin', I owe my darlin',
I owe my darlin' Clementine,

Three bent pennies and a nickel,
Oh my darlin' Clementine.

There she stood beside the bar rail,
Drinking pink gins for two bits,
And the swollen whiskey barrels
Stood in awe beside her tits.

Eyes of whiskey, lips of water
As she sodden at me peer,
Dawns the daylight in her temple
With a fucking-warming leer.

Hung me guitar on the bar rail
At the sweetness of the sign,
In one leap lept out me trousers
Plunged into the foaming brine.

She was bawdy, she was busty
She could match the great Buzoom,
As she strained out of her bloomers
Like a melon tree in bloom.

Oh the oak tree and the cypress
never more together twine,
Since that creeping poison ivy
Laid its blight on Clementine.

44. COCKLES AND MUSSELS

(Sung to the tune of "Molly Malone")

CHORUS:Alive, alive-o, alive, alive-o
Singing cockles and mussels
Alive, alive-o.

In Dublin's fair city where girls are so pretty
I first set my eyes on sweet Molly Malone
As she wheeled her wheel barrow, through streets broad
and narrow

Singing cockles and mussels alive, alive-o.

She was a fishmonger, but sure twas no wonder
For so were her father and mother before
And they each wheeled the barrow, through streets broad
and narrow
Singing cockles and mussels alive, alive-o.

She died of a fever and no one could save her
And that was the end of sweet Molly Malone
Her ghost wheels her barrow, through streets broad and
narrow
Singing cockles and mussels alive, alive-o.

45. COME JUG, MY HONEY, LET'S TO BED

John. Come *Jug*, my Honey, let's to bed,
It is no Sin, sin we are wed;
For when I am near thee by desire,
I burn like any Coal of Fire.
Jug. To quench thy Flames I'll soon agree,
Thou art the Sun, and I the Sea;
All Night within my Arms shalt be,
And rise each Morn as fresh as he.
CHO. *Come on then, and couple together,*
Come all, the Old and the Young,
The Short and the Tall;
The richer than Croesus,
And poorer than Job,
For 'tis Wedding and Bedding,
That Peoples the Globe.
John. My Heart and all's at thy command,
And tho' I've never a Foot of Land,
Yet six fat Ewes, and one milch Cow,
I think, my *Jug*, is Wealth enow.

Jug. A Wheel, six Platters and a Spoon,
A Jacket edg'd with blue Galloon;
My Coat, my Smock is thine, and shall
And something under best of all.

46. COURT OF THE HORNY FIVE
SWEETHEART SONG

CHORUS: In the mood, hard on crazy rhythm,
In the mood, hard on crazy rhythm,
In the mood, hard on crazy rhythm,
Up tight, and out of sight, and in the mood.

She's got nipples on her tits just as big as your thumb.
She's jot somethin' 'tween her legs to make a dead man
cum.
She's got shoo-fly pie - apple pandowdy,
Makes your balls rise up and makes your pecker say
"Howdy"'.
You can huff and you can puff and you can strut your stuff,
But you can't eat enough of her wonderful muff!

Oh, the nipples on her tits are as big as my thumb.
The wiggle of her ass will make a dead man cum.
She's a mean mother fucker and a great cocksucker.
She's my girl; she fucks.

47. COURTIN' IN THE KITCHEN

CHORUS:Tooral ooral ooral a, tooral ooral addy,
Tooral ooral ooral ooral a, tooral ooral addy.

Come single belle and beau, unto me pay attention,
Don't ever fall in love for 'tis the devil's own invention.
Once I fell in love with a maiden so bewitchin',

Miss Henrietta Bell out of Captain Kelly's kitchen.

At the age of seventeen I was 'prenticed to a grocer,
Not far from Stephen's Green where Miss Henry used to go,
Sir.
Her manners were sublime, she set me heart a twitchin',
And she invited me to a hooley in the kitchen.

Next Sunday being the day we were to have the flare up,
I dressed meself quite gay, an' I frizzed and oiled my hair up.
The captain had n-o wife, faith, he had gone out fishing,
So we kicked up high life down below stairs on the kitchen.

Just as the clock struck six we sat down to the table,
She handed tea and cake and I ate while I was able.
I drank hot punch and tea till me sides had got a stitch in,
And the hours passed quick away with the courtin' in the
kitchen.

With me arms around her waist she slyly hinted marriage,
To the door in dreadful haste came Captain Kelly's carriage
Her eyes soon filled with hate and poison she was spitting,
When the Captain at the door walked straight into the
kitchen.

She flew up off my knees, full five feet up or higher,
And over head and heels, threw me slap into the fire.
My new Repealer's coast, that I bought from Mr. Mitchell,
With a twenty shilling note, went to blazes in the kitchen.

I grieved to see my duds, all smeared with soot and ashed,
When a tub of dirty suds, right in my face she dashed.
As I lay on the floor and the water she kept pitchin',
The footman broke the door, and marched down into the
kitchen.

When the Captain came downstairs, tho' he saw my
situation,
In spite of all my prayers, I was marched off to the station.

For me they'd take no bail, tho' to get home I was itchin',
But I had to tell the tale, how I came into the kitchen.

I said she did invite me but she gave a flat denial,
For assault she did indict me and I was sent to trial.
She swore I robbed the house in spite of all her screetchin',
And I got six months hard for me courtin' in the kitchen.

48. DAISY

(Sung to the tune of "Daisy")

Daisy, Daisy,
Give me your answer do.
I'm half crazy,
Six inches into you.
It won't be a stylish entry,
I can't afford a frenchie.
But you'll look sweet,
Between the sheets,
When I'm six inches into you.

49. DARKIE SUNDAY SCHOOL

CHORUS:Young folk, old folk, everybody come
To the darkie Sunday School
And we'll have lots of fun
Bring your sticks of chewing gum
And sit upon the floor
And we'll tell you Bible stories
That you've never heard before.

Now Adam was the first man
So we're led to believe
He walked into the garden
And bumped right into Eve
There was no one there to show him
But he quickly found the way
And that's the very reason

Why we're singing here today.

The Lord said unto Noah
"It's going to rain today"
So Noah built a bloody great Ark
In which to sail away,
The animals went in two by two
But soon got up to tricks
So, although they came in two by two
They came out six by six.

Now Moses in the bullrushes
Was all wrapped up in swathe
Pharaoh's daughter found him
When she went down there to bathe
She took him back to Pharaoh
And said, "I found him on the shore"
And Pharaoh winked his eye and said
"I've heard that one before.

King Solomon and King David
Lived most immoral lives
Spent their time a-chasing
After other people's wives
The Lord spake unto both of them
And it worked just like a charm
'Cos Solomon wrote the Proverbs
And David wrote the Psalms.

Now Samson was an Israelite
And very big and strong
Delilah was a Philistine
Always doing wrong
They spent a week together

50. DEPARTMENT STORE

Chorus :_
I used to work in Chicago, in a department store,
I used to work in Chicago, but I don't work there anymore.

A lady came in the hatshop,
"What kind would you like?" I said,
"Felt," she said, Felt her I did,
I'll never work there anymore.
Chorus

A lady came in for gloves one day,
"What kind would you like?" I said,
"Rubber," She said, rubber I did,
I'll never work there anymore.
Chorus

ŠA lady came in for a sweater one day,
"What kind would you like?" I said,
"Jumper," She said, jump 'er I did,
I'll never work there anymore.
Chorus

A lady came in for a cake one day,
"What kind would you like?" I said,
"Layer," She said, lay 'er I did,
I'll never work there anymore.
Chorus

A lady came for a ticket one day,
"Where would you like to go?"
"Bangor," She said, bang 'er I did,
I'll never work there anymore.
Chorus

51. DIAMOND LILY

Oh her name is Diamond Lily
She's a whore in Piccadilly,
And her brother has a brothel in the Strand,
Her father sells his arse hole
At the Elephant and Castle,
They're the richest fucking family in the land.

There's a man deep in a dungeon
With his hand upon his prick
And the shadow of his prick upon the wall
And the ladies as they pass
Stick their hat-pins up his arse,
And the little mice play billiards with his balls.

There's a little green urinal
To the north of Waterloo
And another a little further up,
There's a member of the army
Playing tunes upon his dick
While the passers-by put pennies in his cup.

52. DID YOU EVER SEE

CHORUS:Did you ever see,
Did you ever see,
Did you ever see,
Such a funny thing before.

Oh, I got an Aunty Sissy,
And she's only got one titty,
But it's very long and pointed
And the nipple's double jointed.

I've got a cousin Daniel,
And he's got a cockerspaniel,
If you tickled 'im in the middle

He would lift his leg and piddle.

Oh, I've got a cousin Rupert,
He plays outside center for Newport,
The think so much about him
That they always play without him.

Oh, I've got a cousin Anna,
And she's got a grand piana,
And she ram aram arama,
Till the neighbors say "God Damn Her."

53. DINAH DINAH SHOW US YOUR LEG

CHORUS:Dinah Dinah show us your leg, show us you leg,
show us your leg,
Dinah Dinah show us your leg a yard above your knee

Alternative substitute Lulu for Dinah
CHORUS:Oh gang bang Dinah, Dinah's goin' away.
Who we gonna gang bang, when Dinah's gone away?

Some girls work in factories,
Some girls work in stores,
But my girl works in a whorehouse,
With forty other whores.

I took her to the pictures,
We sat down in the stalls,
And every time the lights went out,
She grabbed me by the balls.

She and I went fishing,
In a dainty punt,
And every time I hooked a fish,
She stuffed it up her cunt.

I wish I was a silver ring,

Upon my Dinah's hand,
And everytime she scratched her cunt,
I'd see the promised land.

Dinah had a puppy,
Dinah had a duck,
She put them in the bathtub,
To see if they would fuck.

A rich girl has a bra,
A poor girl uses string,
but Dinah uses neither,
She lets the bastards swing.

A rich girl has a ring of gold,
A poor girl one of brass,
The only ring that Dinah has,
Is the one around her ass.

A rich girl uses Vaseline,
A poor girl uses lard,
Dinah uses axle-grease,
Because her cunt's so hard.

Dinah had a baby,
It was an awful shock,
She couldn't call it Dinah 'cos,
The bastard had a cock.

A rich girl uses Kotex,
A poor girl a sheet,
Dinah uses nothing at all,
It dribbles in the street.

Dinah had a boyfriend,
His name was Tommy Tucker,
He took her to the bushes,
To see if he could fuck her.

Dinah met a fisherman,
Fishing for some bass,
Instead of catching fish that day,
He got a piece of ass.

Dinah met a breakaway,
She liked the way he rucked,
The breakaway liked Dinah,
He liked the way she fucked.

Dinah met a scrum half,
Sat down in his lap,
Dinah got the scrum half,
The scrum half got the clap.

Dinah had two boyfriends,
Both named Mitch,
One was a son of a baker,
The other was a son-of-a-bitch.

Dinah met a rugby team,
She liked the way they played,
The team liked Dinah,
They liked the way she laid.

A rich girl drives a limousine,
A poor girl drives a truck,
But the only ride that Dinah has,
Is when she has a Fuck.

A rich girl uses tampons,
A poor girl uses rags,
Dinah uses nothing at all,
Or shoves up burlap bags.

I wish I was a chamber pot,
Under Dinah's bed,
And every time she took a piss,
I'd see her maidenhead.

54. DINAH more verses

A rich girl rides a limousine,
A poor girl rides a truck,
But the only ride that Dinah gets,
Is when she has a fuck.

Chorus ;
 Dinah, Dinah, show us your leg,
 Show us your leg, show us your leg,
 Dinah, Dinah, show us your leg,
 A yard above your knee.

A rich girl wears a brassiere,
A poor girl uses string,
But Dinah uses nothing at all,
She lets the bastards swing.
 Chorus

A rich girl uses vaseline,
A poor girl uses lard,
But Dinah uses axle grease,
Because her cunt's so hard.
 Chorus

A rich girl uses a sanitary towel,
A poor girl uses a sheet,
But Dinah uses nothing at all,
It trails along the street.
 Chorus

A rich girl wears a ring of gold,
A poor girl one of brass,
But the only ring that Dinah has,
Is the one around her arse.
 Chorus

55. DO YOURS HANG LOW?

(Sung to the tune of "Do Your Ears Hang Low")

Do your balls hang low?
Do they dangle to and fro?
Can you tie them in a knot?
Can you tie them in a bow?
Can you sling 'em o'er your shoulder
Like a Continental Soldier?
Do your balls hang low?

56. DOGGIES MEETING

The doggies held a meeting, they came from near and far,
Some came by motor-cycle, and some by motor car.
Each doggy passed the doorway,
Eeach doggie signed the book,
And then unshipped his arsehole, and hung it on a hook.
One dog was not invited, it sorely raised his ire,
He ran into the meeting, and loudly shouted, "FIRE !"
It threw them in confusion, and without a second look,
Each grabbed another's arsehole, from off another hook.

And that's the reason why, sir, when walking down the
street,
And that's the reason why, sir, when doggies chance to
meet,
And that's the reason why, sir, on land or sea or foam,
He will sniff another's arsehole, to see if it's his own.

57. DONT SAY NO

(Chanted)

Oh, my darlin', don't say no,
Onto the sofa you must go.
Up with your petticoat,
Down with your drawers,
You tickle mine

And I'll tickle yours.

58. DRIVE IT ON

I gave her inches ONE and drove it on,
I gave her inches ONE and drove it on,
I gave her inches ONE, she said, "Honey, this is fun,
Put your belly close to mine and drive it on."

I gave her inches TWO and drove it on,
I gave her inches TWO and drove it on,
I gave her inches TWO, she said, "Honey, I love you,
Put your belly close to mine and drive it on."

THREE... "Honey, please fuck me !"
FOUR.... "Honey, give me more !"
FIVE.... "Honey, I'm alive !"
SIX..... "Honey, this is kicks !"
SEVEN... "Honey, this is heaven !"
EIGHT... "Honey, this is great !"
NINE.... "Honey, this is fine !"
TEN..... "Honey, come again !"

59. ESKIMO NELL

(Recited)

Gather round all you whorey
Gather round and hear this story.
When a man rows old, & his balls grow cold
And the tip of his prick turns blue,
It bends in the middle like a 1 string fiddle
He can tell you a tale or two.

So pull up a chair, and stand me a drink
And a tale to you I'll tell
Of Dead-eye Dick and Mexican Pete,
And a harlot called Eskimo Nell.

When Dead-eye Dick and Mexican Pete
Go forth in search of fun
It's Dead-eye Dick that slings the prick
And Mexican Pete the gun.

When Dead-eye Dick and Mexican Pete
Are sore, depressed and sad
It's always a cunt that bears the brunt
Bat the shooting ain't so bad.

Now Dead-eye Dick and Mexican Pete
Live down by Dead Man's Creek
And such was their luck they'd had no fuck
For nigh on half a week.

Just a moose or two and a caribou,
And a bison cow or so,
And for Dead-eye Dick with his kingly prick
This fucking was mighty slow.

So do or dare this horny pair
Set forth for the Rio Grande,
Dead-eye Dick with his mighty prick
And Pete with his gun in his hand.

And as they blazed their noisy trail
No man their path withstood,
And many a bride, her husband's pride
A pregnant widow stood.

They reached the strand of the Rio Grande
At the height of a blazing noon,
And to slack their thirst and do their worst
They sought Black Mike's Saloon.

And as they pushed the great doors wide
Both prick and gun flashed free.
According to sex, you bleeding wrecks,

You drink or fuck with me."

They'd heard of Dead-eye Dick,
From Maine to Panama
So with scarcely worse than a muttered cur
Those dagos sought the bar.

The girls too knew his playful ways
Down on the Rio Grande,
And forty whores pulled down their drawer
At Dead-eye Dick's command.

They saw the fingers of Mexican Pete
Itch on the trigger grip
And they didn't wait, at fearful rate
Those whores began to strip.

Now Dead-eye Dick was breathing quick
With lecherous snorts and grunts
So forty arses were bared to view
And likewise forty cunts.

Now forty cunts and forty arses
If you can use your wits,
And if you're slick at arithmetic,
Makes exactly eighty tits.

Now eighty tits are a gladsome sight
For a man with a raging stand
It may be rare in Berkeley Square
But not on the Rio Grande.

Now Dead-eye Dick had fucked a few
On the last preceding night,
This he had done just to show his fun
And to wet his appetite.

His phallic limb was in fucking trim,
As he backed and took a run

He made a dart at the nearest tart
And scored a hole in one.

He bore her to the sandy floor
And there he fucked her fine
And though she grinned
It put the wind up the other thirty-nine.

When Dead-eye Dick lets loose his prick
He's got no time to spare,
For speed & length combined with strength
He fairly singes hair.

He made a dart at the next spare tart,
When into that harlot's hell
Strode a gentle maid who was unafraid,
And her name it was Eskimo Nell.

By this time Dick had got his prick
Well into number two
When Eskimo Nell let out a yell,
She bawled to him, "Hey you."

He gave a flick of his muscular prick
And the girl flew over his head,
And he wheeled about with an angry shout.
His face and his prick were red.

She glanced our hero up and down,
His looks she seemed to decry,
With utter scorn she glimpsed the horn
That rose from his hairy thigh.

She blew the smoke from her cigarette
Over his steaming knob
So utterly beat was Mexican Pete
He failed to do his job.

It was Eskimo Nell who broke the spell

In accents clear and cool,
"You cunt struck shrimp of a Yankee pimp.
You call that thing a tool?"

"If this here town can't take that down,"
She sneered to those cowering whores,
"There's one little cunt can do the stunt,
It's Eskimo Nell's, not yours."

She stripped her garments one by one
With an air of conscious pride
And as she stood in her womanhood
They saw the great divide.

She seated herself on a table top
Where someone had left his glass,
With a twitch of her tits she crushed it to bits
Between the cheeks of her arse.

She flexed her knees with supple ease,
And spread her legs apart,
With a friendly nod to the mangy sod
She gave him the cue to start.

But Dead-eye Dick knew a trick or two,
He meant to take his time,
And a girl like this was fucking bliss
So he played the pantomime.

He flexed his arse hole to and fro
And made his balls inflate
Until they looked like granite knobs
Up on a garden gate.

He blew his anus inside out,
His balls increased in size,
His mighty prick grew twice as thick
Till it almost reached his eyes.

He polished it up with alcohol,
And made it steaming hot
To finish the job he sprinkled the knob
With a cayenne pepperpot.

Then neither did he take a run
Nor did he take a leap,
Nor did he stoop, but took a swoop
And a steady forward creep.

With piercing eye he took a sight
Along his mighty tool,
And the steady grin as he pushed it in
Was calculatedly cool.

Have you seen the giant pistons
On the mighty C.P.R.
With the driving force of a thousand horse.
Well, you know what pistons are.

Or you think you do. But you've yet to learn
The ins and outs of the trick
Of the work that's done on a non-stop run
By a guy like Dead-eye Dick.

But Eskimo Nell was no infidel,
As good as whole harem
With the strength of ten in her abdomen
And the rock of ages between.

Amid stops she could take the stream
Like the flush of a watercloset,
And she gripped his cock like a Yale Lock
On the National Safe Deposit.

But Dead-eye Dick could not come quick,
He meant to conserve his powers,
If he'd a mind he'd grind and grind
For a couple of solid hours.

Nell lay for a while with a subtle smile,
The grip of her cunt grew keener,
Squeezing her thigh she sucked him dry
With the ease of a vacuum cleaner.

She performed this trick in a way so slick
As to set in complete defiance
The basic cause and primary laws
That govern sexual science.

She calmly rode through the phallic code
Which for years had stood the test,
And the ancient rules of the classic schools
In a second or two went West.

And so my friends we come to the end
Of copulation's classic
The effect on Dick was sudden and quick
And akin to an anesthetic.

He fell to the floor, and knew no more
His passions extinct and dead
And he did not shout as his prick fell out
Though 'twas stripped right down to a thread

Then Mexican Pete jumped to his feet
To avenge his pal's affront,
With jarring jolt of his blue-nosed Colt
He rammed it up her cunt.

He rammed it up to the trigger grip
And fired three times three
But to his surprise she closed her eyes
And smiled in ecstasy.

She jumped to her feet with a smile so sweet
"Bully", she said, "for you.
Though I had guessed that was the best

That you two poor cocks could do."

"When next, my friend, that you intend
To sally forth for fun
Buy Dead-eye Dick a sugar stick
And yourself an elephant gun.

"I'm going back to the frozen North,
Where the pricks are hard and strong.
Back to the land of the frozen stand
Where the nights are six months long.

"It's hard as tin when they put it in
In the land where spunk is spunk
Not a trickling stream of lukewarm cream
But a solid frozen chunk.

"Back to the land where they understand
What it means to fornicate,
Where even the dead sleep two in a bed
And the babies masturbate.

"Back to the land of the grinding gland,
Where the walrus plays with his prong,
Where the polar bear wanks off in his lair
That's where they'll sing this song.

"They'll tell this tale on the Arctic Trail
Where the nights are sixty below,
Where it's so damn cold that the Johnnies are sold
Wrapped up in a ball of snow.

"In the valley of death with baited breath
That's where they'll sing it too,
Where the skeletons rattle in sexual battle,
And the rotting corpses screw.

"Back to the land where men are men,
Terra Bellicum,

And there I'll spend my worthy end
For the North is calling: 'Come."'

So Dead-eye Dick and Mexican Pete
Slunk out of the Rio Grande,
Dead-eye Dick with his useless prick
And Pete with no gun in his hand.

60. EYES RIGHT
(Chanted)

Eyes right,
Skin back tight,
Bollocks to the front.
We're the boys who make no noise,
When we go hunting cunt.
We're the riders of the night,
And we'd rather fuck than fight.
We're the riders of the (your team's name) RFC.

61. FA LA LA

CHORUS:Fa la la la la la la la la la la la la la la la la la la
Fa la la la la la la la la la la la la la la la la la.

I'll be up your flue in a minute or two,
'Cause I know where to find it.
It's around the front and it's called the cunt,
And the asshole's right behind it.

My darling Grace, I love your face,
I love you in your nightie.
When the moonlight flits across your tits,
Oh, Jesus Christ Almighty.

I'll be up your gash as quick as a flash,
'Cause I am Jack the Ripper.

Though some have hairs -and some are bald,
But they all smell like a kipper.

I'll be between your thighs despite your lies,
Because you love me deary.
I'll be up and down and in and out,
Until you are too weary.

You'll be on your knees and begging please,
Because you are so horny.
I'll be round about and up your spout,
And gone before the morning.

The very best time I ever had,
Is when I take out Lucy.
'Cause after we dine and after we dance,
I get to eat her pussy.

62. FA LA LA LA LA

Christmas comes but once a year,
Fa-la-la-la-la, la la la la
If that was me I'd turn quite queer,
Fa-la-la-la-la, la la la la
Christmas is the time for fucking,
Fa-la-la-la-la, la la la la
Give your end a fucking good ducking,
Fa-la-la-la-la, la la la la

Paint your balls with grease and lacquer,
Fa-la-la-la-la, la la la la
What joy to have a slippery knacker,
Fa-la-la-la-la, la la la la
My woman shouts in gay abandon,
Fa-la-la-la-la, la la la la
"Cock's not enough so slip the lot in !"
Fa-la-la-la-la, la la la la

Hoist her arse and wiggle your hips,

a-la-la-la-la, la la la la
Bend your neck and nibble her tits,
Fa-la-la-la-la, la la la la
And when she writhes in fits of passion,
Fa-la-la-la-la, la la la la
Ejaculate and slip her your ration,
Fa-la-la-la-la, la la la la

When you're done, roll over and snore,
Fa-la-la-la-la, la la la la
But she ain't pleased 'cos she wants more,
Fa-la-la-la-la, la la la la
You peer down at your old John Thomas,
Fa-la-la-la-la, la la la la
The wrinkled old sod's had enough this Christmas,
Fa-la-la-la-la, la la la la

So plug in your pneumatic drill, Fa-la-la-la-la, la la la la
Guaranteed to give her a thrill,
Fa-la-la-la-la, la la la la
And while she revels in self abuse,
Fa-la-la-la-la, la la la la
You wonder why your root hangs loose,
Fa-la-la-la-la, la la la la

63. FANNY BAY

If you ever go across the sea to Darwin,
Then maybe at the closing of the day,
You will see the local harlots
at their business,
And watch the sun go down on Fanny Bay.

Some are black and some are white,
And some are brindle,
And some are young
and some are old and grey,
But what will cost you twenty quid

in Lower Crown Street,
Will cost you half a zac in Fanny Bay.

64. FARMER'S DAUGHTER

CHORUS: I had her, I had her, I had her away.
I had her, I had her, I had her away.
(Repeat last two lines of each verse.)

I knew a farmer and I knew him well.
He had a daughter and her name was Nell.
She was so pretty and only sixteen,
When I showed her the works of my Thrashing Machine.

The barn door was open and I stepped inside.
Off in the comer so softly I spied.
She worked the throttle and I worked the steam,
As I showed her the works of my Thrashing Machine.

Well, three months went by and all was not well.
Something had happened to our little Nell.
For under her pinny could clearly be seen,
The diabolical works of my Thrashing Machine.

Now, nine months went by and a doctor was called.
Unto sweet Nellie a baby was born.
And under his nappy could clearly be seen,
A brand new, twin cylinder Thrashing Machine.

65. FOUR OLD WHORES

There were four old whores of Baltimore,
Drinking beer and wine,
The topic of conversation was, "Mine is bigger than thine."

Chorus :
Roly Poly, tickle my holey, smell of of my slimey flue,
Then drag your nuts across my guts,
I'm one of the whorey crew.

The first old whore from Baltimore said,
"Mine's as big as the air,
The birds fly in, the birds fly out, and never tickle a hair."
Chorus

The second old whore from Baltimore said,
"Mine's as big as the moon,
The men jump in, the men jump out,
And never touch the womb."
Chorus

The third old whore from Baltimore said,
"Mine's as big as the sea,
The ships sail in, the ships sail out,
And leave their rigging free."
Chorus

The fourth old whore from Baltimore said,
"Mine's the biggest of all,
The sun could set in the crack of my arse,
Not singeing a hair at all."
Chorus

66. FUCK 'EM ALL

Fuck 'em all, fuck 'em all, fuck 'em all,
The long and the short and the tall,
FUCK all the blond cunts and all the brunets,
Don't be to choosy, just fuck all you gets,
'Cause we're saying goodbye to them all,
As back to the barracks we crawl,
You'll get no erection at short-arm inspection,
So prick up you men, fuck 'em all.

Fuck 'em all, fuck 'em all, fuck 'em all,
The long and the short and the tall,
Fuck all the cunts 'til you break it in two,
You'll get no loving where you're going to,

'Cause we're saying goodbye to them all,
As back to the barracks we crawl,
So get your big prick up and give it a stick up,
Cheer up my lads, fuck 'em all.

67. FUCK HIM

(Chanted)

He ought to be publicly pissed on.
He ought to be publicly shot. Bang! Bang!
And stuffed in a bloody urinal,
To lay there to fester and rot.
So him, him, FUCK HIM!

68. FUCK OFF YOU DRUNKEN GENTLEMAN

Fuck OFF you drunken gentleman, you're in my fucking way,
Got to get home before the start of snowy Christmas day,
My wife is sa - ving herself for some midnight foreplay,
Then its the joining of pussy and cock,
Pussy and cock, then its the joi - ning of pussy and cock.
Fuck OFF yourself you dirty fat cunt, I haven't a fucking care,
What wife would want to shag with you
With a face like a grizzly bear,
I'll bet your foreskin's full of crabs,
The ones that stink and stare,
As you play with your tool and have a wank,
Have a wank, as you play with your tool and have a wank.

My wife has shaved her pubic hairs, she used my razor blade,
She slipped and nicked her clitoris, it made her quite afraid,
So I bent down and kissed it better, when she got laid,
And her orgasm made her moan and shout,
Moan and shout, and her orgasm made her moan and shout.

On Christmas morn I have the horn,
It makes the day complete,
My wife's a vegetarian, she does not eat red meat,
But she forgets this rule and eats my tool, it is a fucking treat,
It's more filling than e - gg and toast,
Egg and toast, it's more fi - lling than e - gg and toast.

Frosty the snowman gets so cold,
His hampton has just shrunk,
There is no hope of unsafe sex, his balls are free from spunk,
He'd love to get his end away, instead he gets quite drunk,
As he stands in the heat and melts his knob,
Melts his knob, as he sta - nds in the heat and melts his knob.

69. GENTLEMEN SHOULD PLEASE REFRAIN

(Sung to the tune of "Poisoning Pigeons in the Park")

Gentlemen should please refrain
From flushing toilets while the train
Is standing in the station for a while.
We encourage contemplation
While the train is in the station,
Cross your legs and grit your teeth and smile.

If you wish to pass some water
You should sing out for a porter
Who will place a basin in the bog;
Tramps and hoboes undeneath
Get it in the eye and teeth,
But that's what comes from being underdog.

Drinking while the train is moving
Is another way of proving,
That control of eye and hand is sure;

We like our clients to be neat,
So please don't wet upon the seat,
Or, even worse, don't splash upon the floor.

If the Ladies' Room be taken,
do not feel the least forsaken,
Never show the sign of sad defeat,
Try the Gents across the hall,
and if some man has felt the call
He'll courteously relinquish you his seat.

If these efforts are in vain,
then simply break the window pane,
This novel method's used by very few,
We go strolling through the park,
a-goosing statues in the dark
If Peter Pan can take it, why can't you?

70. GLORIOUS BEER

(Sung to the tune of "Food" from the opera Oliver)

CHORUS:Beer, beer, glorious beer,
Fill yourself right up to here.
Drink a good deal of it, make a good meal of it.
Stick to your old fashion beer,
Don't be afraid of it, drink till you're made of it.
Now all together a cheer,
Up with sale of it, down with a pale of it.
Glorious, glorious beer.

Now I won't sing of Sherbet and water
For Sherbet and beer will not rhyme
'ne working man can't afford Champagne
It's a bit more than two D a time
So I'll sing you a song of a garle
A garle that I love so dear
I all owe to that grand institution
That beautiful tonic called beer, beer, beer.

It's the daddy of all lubricators
The best thing there is for the neck
Can be used as a gargle or lotion
By persons of every sect
Now we know who the goddess of wine was
But was there a goddess of beer
If so let's drink to her health boys
And wish that we'd got her here, here, here.

So up, up with Brandies and sodas
But down and down with the beer
It's good for you when you're hungry
You can eat it without any fear
So mop up your beer while you're able
Of four-half let's have our fill
And I know you'll all join me in wishing
Good luck to my dear uncle Bill, Bill, Bill.

71. H.A.N.D.

I laid my hand upon her knee, she said,
"Young man you're very very free."

Chorus :
With your hand, with your hand, with your H-A-N-D hand.

So I laid my hand upon her toe, she said,
"Young man, you're very very low."
Chorus

So I put my hand upon her calf, she said,
"Young man you're there by half."
Chorus

So I put my hand upon her thigh, she said,
"Young man you're getting rather high."
Chorus

So I put my hand upon her rear, she said,

"Young man you're getting rather near."
Chorus

So I put my hand upon her bum, she said,
"Young man you'd better use your thumb."
Chorus

So I laid my hand upon her quim, she said,
"Young man you'd better put it in."
Chorus

So I put it in and waggled it about, she said,
"Young man you'd better take it out."
Chorus

So I took it out and wiped it on the grass, she said,
"Young man now stick it up your arse."
Chorus

72. HARLEQUIN'S LAMENT

Scrum halves and centers and forwards, too.
Thumbs up their assholes with fuck-all to do.
Drinking our beer in the company of fools.
May the lord piss on you sideways.
May the lord piss on you sideways.
May the lord piss on you sideways.
'Tis the Harlequin's Lament.

The first thing we ask for, we ask for is beer.
Beautiful, wonderful, glorious beer.
If we can have one beer, why can't we have ten?
Why can't we own a brewery?
Why can't we own a brewery?
Why can't we own a brewery?
'Tis the Harlequin's Lament.

The next thing we ask for, we ask for is girls.
Beautiful, wonderful, glorious girls.

If we can have one girl, why can't we have ten'?
Why can't we own a whorehouse?
Why can't we own a whorehouse?
Why can't we own a whorehouse?
'Tis the Harlequin' s Lament.
The last thing we ask for is boys.

The last thing I ask for is boys.
Beautiful, wonderful, glorious boys.
If we can have one boy, why can't we have ten?
Why can't we own a scout troop?
Why can't we own a scout troop?
Why can't we own a scout troop?
Tis the Harlequin's Lament.

73. HERE'S TO THE SPLIT
(Toast)

Here's to the split that never heals,
The longer you rub it the better it feels.
And all the soap this side of hell,
Can't wash away that fishy smell.

74. HE'S DIRT BASTARD
(Chanted)

For he's a dirty bastard,
Scum of the earth.
Born in a whorehouse.
Shit on, pissed on, shoved around the universe.

Of all the son-of-a-bitches,
he is the worst.
Born down in (city of your choice),
The armpit of the universe.

So him, him, FUCK HIM!

75. HIS FATHER WAS A EUNUCH

(Chanted)

His father was a eunuch,
He had no balls at all.
What could have been the use of him,
Is more than I recall.
Band, Bang, FUCK HIM.

76. HITLER HAS ONLY GOT ONE BALL

CHORUS:Hitler has only got one ball,
Stalin has two, but very small.
Himmler is very similar,
And poor old Goebbels has no balls at all.

We are from (your team's name) RFC.
We are always out to win.
Men, men very strong,
We are the forwards and backs again.

And if the forwards push very hard,
Backs play with all their hearts.
Men, men very strong,
We are the forwards and backs again.

77. HOLD'EM DOWN YOU ZULU WARRIOR

(Sung to the tune of "Zulu Warrior")

Hold 'em down you Zulu Warrior,
Hold'em down you Zulu Chief,
Chief! Chief! Chief! Chief
Ar-Delle zumba zumba zumba.
Ar-Delle zumba zumba zay.
Ar-Delle zumba zumba zumba.
Ar-Delle zumba zumba zay.

78. I DON'T KNOW WHAT HIS NAME IS...

CHORUS:I don't know what his name is and wherever he may be,
   Just listen while I tell you what he did to me!

I went through the front gate
Like a good girl should,
And he slipped round the back way
Like I knew he would.

I went in the front door
Like a good girl should,
And he slipped in behind me
Like I knew he would.

I went up the stairs
Like a good girl should,
And he came up behind me
Like I knew he would.

I went in my bedroom
Like a good girl should,
And he slipped in behind me
Like I hoped he would.

I took all my clothes off
Like a good girl should,
And he took off his trousers
Like I knew he would.

I put on my 'jamas
Like a good girl should,
And then he took them off again
Like I knew he would.

I got into bed
Like a good girl should,
And he got in beside me

Like I knew he would.

I laid on my side
Like a good girl should,
But then he turned me over
Like I knew he would.

FINAL
CHORUS:I don't know what his name is and wherever he may
be,
It's none of your damned business what he did to me!

79. I DON'T WANNA TALK ABOUT IT

CHORUS:I don't wanna talk about it how you broke my
heart.
   If I stay here just a little bit longer,
If I stay here won't you listen to my heart, OH my heart.

I can tell by your eyes that you're probably been crying
forever
And the stars in the sky don't mean nothing to you there a
mirror.

If I stand all along will the shadow hide the color of my heart
Blue for the tears, black for the night spears
And the stars in the sky don't mean nothing to you there a
mirror.

80. I DON'T WANT TO JOIN THE ARMY

CHORUS:I don't want to join the army,
I don't want to go to war.
I'd rather hang around Piccadilly Underground,
Living on the earnings of a high born lady.
I don't want a bayonet up me asshole,
I don't want me balls shot away.

I'd rather stay in England, in merry, merry England,
And fornicate me fucking life away. Go blimey ...

Monday I touched her on the ankle,
Tuesday I touched her on the knee,
And Wednesday, I must confess, I lifted up her dress,
Thursday I saw you know what,
Friday I laid me 'and upon it,
Saturday she gave me balls a twitch, twitch, twitch,
And Sunday after supper, I rammed me fucker up 'er,
And now I'm paying 76 a week. Go blimey ...

SECOND
CHORUS:I don't want to join the Navy.
I don't want to go to sea.
I'd rather hang around Piccadilly Underground,
Living on the earnings of a high born lady.
I don't need no Frenchy women,
London's full of girls I never had.
I want to stay in Blight, Lord Gawd Almighty,
Following in the footsteps of me dad.

81. I LOVE MY WIFE

I love my wife;
I love her truly;
I love the hole
She pisses through.
I love her tits-tittly-tits-tittly-tits
And her nut brown arse hole.
I would eat her shit,
Chomp, chomp, gobble, gobble
With a rusty spoon,
With a rusty spoon.

82. I USED TO WORK IN CHICAGO

CHORUS: I used to work in Chicago
In a department store.
I used to work in Chicago
I did but I don't any more.

A woman came in and asked for a dress,
I asked her what dress she adored,
A jumper she said so jump her I did,
I don't work there anymore.

A woman came in and asked for a card,
I asked her what card she adored,
A poker she said so poke her I did,
I don't work there anymore.

A woman came in and asked for a dog.
I asked her what dog she adored,
A cocker she said so cock her I did,
I don't work there anymore.

A woman came in and asked for some shoes
I asked her what shoes she adored,
A slipper she said so slip her I did,
I don't work there anymore.

A woman came in and asked for a cake,
I asked her what cake she adored,
A layer she said so lay her I did,
I don't work there anymore.

A woman came in and asked for a ball,
I asked her what ball she adored,
A rubber she said so rub her I did,
I don't work there anymore.

A woman came in and asked for some booze
I asked her what booze she adored,
Liquor she said so lick her I did,
I don't work there anymore.

A woman came in and asked for hardware,
I asked her what hardware she adored,
A screw she said so screw her I did,
I don't work there anymore.

A woman came in and asked for a girdle,
I asked her what girdle she adored,
"Rubber!" she said, and rub her I did,
I don't work there anymore.

A woman came in and asked for a pet,
I asked her what pet she adored,
"A pussy!" she said, I took the hint,
I don't work there anymore.

A woman came in and asked for a hat,
I asked her what hat she adored,
"Felt!" she said, so felt her I did,
I don't work there anymore.

A woman came in and asked for a ticket,
I asked her what ticket she adored,
"Bangor!" she said, so bang her I did,
I don't work there anymore.

A woman came in and asked for a dairy,
I asked her what dairy she adored,
"Cream!" she said, so cream her I did,
I don't work there anymore.

83. IF I WERE THE MARRYING KIND

CHORUS:If I were the marrying kind,
Which thank the Lord I'm not sir,
The kind of man that I would be...

...WOULD BE A RUGBY FULLBACK.
I'd find touch, she'd find touch,

We'd both find touch together,
We'd be alright in the middle of the night,
Finding touch together

...WOULD BE A RUGBY HOOKER.
I'd strike hard, she'd strike hard,
We'd both strike hard together,
We'd be alright in the middle of the night, Striking hard
together.

...WOULD BE AN INSIDE CENTER.
I'd pass it out, she'd pass it out,
We'd both pass it out together,
We'd be alright in the middle of the night, Passing it out
together.

...WOULD BE A RUGBY REFEREE.
I'd fuck up, she'd fuck up,
We'd both fuck up together,
We'd be alright in the middle of the night, Fucking up
together.

...WOULD BE A RUGBY PROP.
I'd support a hooker, she'd support a hooker, We'd both
support a hooker together,
We'd be alright in the middle of the night, Supporting a
hooker together.

...WOULD BE A RUGBY FLY-HALF.
I'd whip it out, she'd whip it out,
We'd both whip it out together,
We'd be alright in the middle of the night, Whipping it out
together.

...WOULD BE A RUGBY SCRUM-HALF. I'd put it in, she'd
put it in,
Wed both put it in together,
We'd be alright in the middle of the night, Putting it in
together.

...WOULD BE A RUGBY HALF-TIME ORANGE.
I'd get sucked, she'd get sucked,
We'd both get sucked together,
We'd be alright in the middle of the night,
Getting sucked together.

...WOULD BE A RUGBY SPECTATOR.
I'd come again, she'd come again,
We'd both come again together,
We'd be alright in the middle of the night,
Coming again together.

...WOULD BE A RUGBY SECOND ROW.
I'd push hard, she'd push hard,
Wed both push hard together,
We'd be alright in the middle of the night,
Pushing hard together.

...WOULD BE A RUGBY GROUNDSKEEPER.
I'd trim bush, she'd trim bush,
We'd both trim bush together,
We'd be alright in the middle of the night,
Trimming bush together.

...WOULD BE A RUGBY TICKET TAKER.
I'd punch holes, she'd punch holds,
We'd both punch holes together,
We'd be alright in the middle of the night,
Punching holes together.

...WOULD BE A RUGBY SPECTATOR IN THE RAIN.
I'd wear rubbers, she'd wear rubbers,
We'd both wear rubbers together,
We'd be alright in the middle of the night,
Wearing rubbers together.

... WOULD BE A RUGBY NUMBER EIGHT MAN.
I'd sniff ass, she'd sniff ass,

We'd both sniff ass together,
We'd be alright in the middle of the night,
Sniffing ass together.

...WOULD BE A RUGBY GOAL POST.
I'd stand erect, she'd stand erect,
We'd both stand erect together,
We'd be alright in the middle of the night,
Standing erect together.

...WOULD BE A RUGBY ASSISTANT GROUNDSKEEPER.
I'd fill holes, she'd fill holes,
We'd both fill holes together,
We'd be all right in the middle of the night,
Filling holes together.

...WOULD BE A RUGBY REFEREE'S WHISTLE.
I'd get blown, she'd get blown,
We'd both get blown together,
We'd be alright in the middle of the night,
Getting blown together.

...WOULD BE A RUGBY TOUCH LINE.
I'd get laid, she'd get laid,
We'd both get laid together,
We'd be alright in the middle of the night,
Getting laid Together.

...WOULD BE A RUGBY PARTIER.
I'd keep it up, she'd keep it up,
We'd both keep it up together,
We'd be alright in the middle of the night,
Keeping it up together.

...WOULD BE A RUGBY WING-FORWARD.
I'd come early, she'd come early,
We'd both come early together,
We'd be alright in the middle of the night,
Cumming early together.

...WOULD BE A RUGBY WING.
I'd go hard, she'd go hard,
We'd both go hard together,
We'd be alright in the-middle of the night,
Going hard together.

...WOULD BE ANOTHER RUGBY WING.
I'd never get it, she'd never get it,
We'd both never get it together,
We'd be alright in the middle of the night,
Never getting it together.

...WOULD BE A RUGBY SECOND ASSISTANT
GROUNDSKEEPER.
I'd sow seeds, she'd sow seeds,
We'd both sow seeds together,
We'd be alright in the middle of the night,
Sowing seeds together.

...WOULD BE A RUGBY SPECTATOR FROM 100 MILES
AWAY.
I'd eat out, she'd eat out,
We'd both eat out together,
We'd be alright in the middle of the night,
Eating out together.

...WOULD BE A RUGBY BOOT.
I'd come in a box, she'd come in a box,
We'd both come in a box together,
We'd be alright in the middle of the night,
Coming in a box together.

...WOULD BE A RUGBY FULLBACK NUMBER TWO.
I'd kick balls, she'd kick balls,
We'd both kick balls together,
We'd be alright in the middle of the night,
Kicking balls together.

84. I'M A GENTLEMAN OF LEISURE, OF NOBILITY, AND PLEASURE

CHORUS:Ball of yarn, ball of yarn,
I've a mind to spin
your little ball of yarn,
Ball of yarn, ball of yarn,
I've a mind to spin
your little ball of yarn.

I'm a gentleman of leisure, of nobility and pleasure,
With manners of the manor and the morals of the barn,
And when I met a lady in the forest green and shady,
I asked if I could spin her ball of yarn.

She gave her kind consent and behind the bush we went,
And I said: "My dear, there's no cause for alarm."
So I laid her on the ground and with expertise so sound,
I went on to spin her little ball of yarn.

It was nine months after that in my manor where I sat,
I saw a figure coming past the barn,
And a big man with a truncheon quite disturbed my Sunday luncheon,
was father of a little ball of yarn.

85. I'M YOUR MAILMAN

I feel happy, I feel gay
Cause I come twice a day.
I'm your mailman.

I don't mess with keys on locks,
I just stick it in your box.
I'm your mailman.

I can come in any kind of weather,
For you see my bag is made of leather.

I'm your mailman.

Oh! Pat you knockers, ring your chimes,
For you see mine is fine.
I'm your mailman,
With the longest route in town.

86. IN DULUTH

CHORUS:In Duluth, In Duluth
In D', in D', in D', in Duluth,

(Repeat last two lines of each verse)

Oh the eagles they fly high in Duluth.
Oh the eagles they fly high in Duluth.
Oh the eagles they fly high and they shit right in your eye,
Thank the Lord that cows don't fly in Duluth.

There's a man by the name of Hunt in Duluth.
There's a man by the name of Hunt in Duluth.
There's a man by the name of Hunt and he thought he had a cunt,
But his arse was back to front in Duluth.

There's a shortage of good bogs in Duluth.
There's a shortage of good bogs in Duluth.
There's a shortage of good bogs so they wait until it clogs,
Then they saw it off in logs in Duluth.

There's a shortage of bogpaper in Duluth.
There's a shortage of bogpaper in Duluth.
Mere's a shortage of bogpaper so they wait until it's vapor,
Then they light it with a taper in Duluth.

There's a man by the name of Smith in Duluth.
There's a man by the name of Smith in Duluth.
There's a man by the name of Smith and he thinks that he can't sniff,

Foul odor from the syph in Duluth.

Oh they teach the babies tricks in Duluth.
Oh they teach the babies tricks in Duluth.
Oh they teach the babies tricks and by the time that they are six,
The suck their father's pricks in Duluth.

It's a fuck of a situation in Duluth.
It's a fuck of a situation in Duluth.
It's a fuck of a situation and they're sunk in masturbation,
For there ain't no fornication in Duluth.

There's a shortage of good whores in Duluth.
There's a shortage of good whores in Duluth.
There's a shortage of good whores but there's keyholes in the doors,
And there's knotholes in the floors in Duluth.

There's a man by the name of Best in Duluth.
There's a man by the name of Best in Duluth.
There's a man by the name of Best and he thought he had a breast,
But his balls were on his chest in Duluth.

There's a girl by the name of Doris in Duluth.
There's a girl by the name of Doris in Duluth.
There's a girl by the name of Doris and her boyfriend's name is Horace,
And he tickles her clitoris in Duluth.

Oh the vicar is a bugger in Duluth.
Oh the vicar is a bugger in Duluth.
Oh the vicar is a bugger and the curate is another,
So they bugger one another in Duluth.

There's a whore called Dirty Dinah in Duluth.
There's a whore called Dirty Dinah in Duluth.

There's a whore called Dirty Dinah and they say there's nothing finer,
Than a trip up her vagina in Duluth.

There's a man by the name of Brock in Duluth.
There's a man by the name of Brock in Duluth.
There's a man by the name of Brock with a multi-colored cock,
Like a stick of candy rock in Duluth.

Oh the girls they wear tin pants in Duluth.
Oh the girls they wear tin pants in Duluth.
Oh the girls they wear tin pants but they take them off to dance,
Everybody gets a chance in Duluth.

There's a knot hole in the floor in Duluth.
There's a knot hole in the floor in Duluth.
There's a knot hole in the floor and we use it for a whore,
There's some cocks that are sore in Duluth.

Oh a seagull saw a lighthouse in Duluth.
Oh a seagull saw a lighthouse in Duluth.
Oh a seagull saw a lighthouse and he thought it was a shithouse,
Now the lighthouse is a white house in Duluth.

Oh the ladies have big tits in Duluth.
Oh the ladies have big tits in Duluth.
Oh the ladies have big tits and they hang down to their clits,
And we munch them all to bits in Duluth.

87. IN MOBILE

All the eagles they fly high in Mobile, (mow-beel)
repeat
All the eagles they fly high, and they shit right in your eye,
Its a good job cows don't fly in Mobile.

Chorus ;_
 In Mobile, in Mobile, in mo,
 in mo, in mo, in Mobile,
 (repeat last 2 lines of verse)

All the seagulls have a lighthouse in Mobile,
repeat
All the seagulls have a lighthouse
and they use it as a shitehouse,
Now the lighthouse is a whitehouse in Mobile.
 Chorus

There's a shortage of good whores in Mobile,
repeat
There's a shortage of good whores,
But there's keyholes in the doors,
And there's knotholes in the floors in Mobile.
 Chorus

There's a shortage of bogpaper in Mobile,
repeat
There's a shortage of bogpaper, so they wait until it's
vapour,
And they light it with a taper in Mobile.
 Chorus

There's a shortage of san(itary) towels in Mobile,
repeat
There's a shortage of san towels, so they wait until it fouls,
And then dig it out with trowels in Mobile.
 Chorus

Oh the Vicar is a bugger in Mobile,
repeat
Oh the Vicar is a bugger, but the Curate is another,
So they bugger one another in Mobile.
 Chorus

There's a Jew by the name of Cohen in Mobile,

repeat
There's a Jew by the name of Cohen,
To the Christian Church he's going,
'Cos his foreskin keeps on growing in Mobile.
 Chorus

88. IN THE SHADE OF THE OLD APPLE TREE

In the shade of the old apple tree
A pair of fine legs I did see
With some hair at the top
And a little red spot
It looked like a cherry to me.

I pulled out my pride of New York
It fitted it just like a cork
I said, "Darlin' don't scream
While I fill you with cream
In the shade of the old apple tree."

And as we both lay on the grass
With my two hands around her fat ass
She said, "If you'll be true
You can have fuck too!
In the shade of the old apple tree."

89. INCEST TIME IN TEXAS

(Sung to the tune of "The Yellow Rose Of Texas")

When it's incest time in Texas
And your father is out of town,
Your mother is in the bathroom
With her panties halfway down,
No time for masturbation,
No time to beat your meat,

When it's incest time in Texas
Motherfuckin' can't be beat!

90. INSIDE THOSE RED PLUSH BREECHES

CHORUS:Inside those red plush breeches,
Inside those red plush breeches,
Inside those red plush breeches,
That kept John Thomas warm.

John Thomas was a servant tall
Pride and joy of the servants' hall,
Although he only had one ball,
Inside his red plush breeches.

Of all the servants at the servants' post,
Mary was the one he loved the most,
And she'd keep her hands as was as toast,
Inside his red plush breeches.

Mary had an illegit
awful green and face like shit,
And every time she looked at it,
She cursed those red plush breeches.

Now Mary laid poor John a trap,
And he fell for it like a sap,
And now he's got a dose of clap,
inside those red plush breeches.

91. IT'S THE SAME THE WHOLE WORLD OVER

CHORUS:It's the same the whole world over; it's the poor what
gets the blame;

It's the rich what gets the gravy; ain't it all a fucking shame.
(or)
It's the same the whole world over; it's the pack which gets the blame;
It's the backs who get the glory; ain't it all a fucking shame.
She was poor but she was honest,
Victim of a rich man's whim,
First he fucked her, then he left her
And she had a child by him.

See him with his hounds and horses,
See him strutting at his club,
While the victim of his wenching
Sips her gin inside a pub.

Then she came to London City,
Just to hide her bleeding shame,
But a politician fucked her
And put her on the streets again.

See him in the House of Commons,
Passing laws to combat crime,
While the victim of his evil
Walks the streets at night in shame.

See him riding in a carriage,
Past the gutter where she stands,
He has made a stylish marriage
At the mercy of syphilitic hands.

See him sitting at the theatre,
In the front row with the best,
While the girl that he has ruined
Entertains a sordid guest.

She him seated in his Rolls Royce,
Driving homeward from the hunt,
He got riches from his marriage
She got sores upon her cunt.

See her stand in Piccadilly,
Offering up her aching quim,
She is now completely ruined
And the cause of all is him.

It was on the bridge at midnight,
Throwing shitballs at the moor,
She said 'Sir, I'm still a virgin."
But she spoke too fucking soon.

It was on the bridge at midnight,
Squeezing blackheads from her crotch,
She said, "Sir, I've still not had it."
He said, "No, not fucking much!"

See her on the bridge at midnight,
Looking down with-baited breath,
"A plague upon all cowards,"
She cried falling to her death.

It was on the bridge at midnight,
Where the rich man met his fate,
Her curse had found her coward
And he was doomed to masturbate.

They dragged her from the river,
Water from her clothes the wrung,
They thought that she was drowned
Till her corpse got up and sung.

Then there came a wealthy pimp,
Marriage was the tale he told,
She had no one else to take her
So she sold her soul for gold.

In a little country cottage,
There her grieving parents live,

Though they the fizz she sends them
Yet they never will forgive.

92. IVAN SCAVINSKY SCAVAR

(Sung to the tune of "Ivan Scavinsky Scavar")

The harems of Egypt are fine to behold;
The harlots the fairest of fair,
But the fairest of all,
Was owned by a sheik named,
Abdul Abulbul Amir.

A traveling brothel
Came down from the north,
'Twas run privately for the Czar,
Who wagered no one could out shag,
Ivan Scavinsky Scavar.

A day was arranged for the spectacle great,
A holiday proclaimed by the Czar,
And the streets were all lined
With the harlots assigned to,
Ivan Scavinsky Scavar.

Old Abdul came in with a snatch by his side,
His eye bore a leer of desire,
And he started to brag
How he would out shag,
Ivan Scavinsky Scavar.

All hairs were shorn and no frenchies were worn,
And this suited Abdul by far,
And he's quite set his mind
On a fast action grind to beat,
Ivan Scavinsky Scavar.

They met on the track with prick at the slack,
A starter's gun punctured the air,
They were both quick to rise,

The crowd gaped at the size of,
Abdul Abulbul Amir.

They worked all the night in the pale yellow light,
Old Abdul he reved like a car,
But he couldn't compete
With the slow steady beat of,
Ivan Scavinsky Scavar.

So Ivan he won and he shouldered his gun,
He bent down to polish the pair,
When something red hot
Up his back passage shot,
'Twas Abdul Abulbul Amir.

The harlots turned green,
The crowd shouted "Queen,"
They were ordered apart by the Czar,
'Twas bloody bad luck for Abdul was stuck up,
Ivan Scavinsky Scavar.

The cream of the joke came when they broke,
'Twas laughed at for years by the Czar,
For Abdul the fool
Left half his tool up
Ivan Scavinsky Scavar.

93. JACK AND JILL

(Sung to the tune of "Jack and Jill")

Jack and Jill went up the hill
To fetch a pail of water.
Jill came down with half a crown
But not for fetching water.

94. JESUS SAVES

(Sung to the tune of "Battle Hymn of the Republic")

CHORUS: Free beer for all the workers.
Free beer for all the workers.
Free beer for all the workers,
'Till the red revolution begins.

Jesus puts His money in the Bank of Montreal,
Jesus puts His money in the Bank of Montreal,
Jesus puts His money in the Bank of Montreal,
Jesus saves, Jesus saves, Jesus saves.

Jesus plavs goalie for the Toronto Maple Leafs,
Jesus plays goalie for the Toronto Maple Leafs,
Jesus plays goalie for the Toronto Maple Leafs,
Jesus saves, Jesus saves, Jesus saves.

Jesus walks on water, He's the lifeguard at our pool,
Jesus walks on water, He's the lifeguard at our pool,
Jesus walks on water, He's the lifeguard at our pool,
Jesus saves, Jesus saves, Jesus saves.

Jesus makes a Trojan cause I used one last night,
Jesus makes a Trojan cause I used one last night,
Jesus makes a Trojan cause I used one last night,
Jesus saves, Jesus saves, Jesus saves.

Jesus He sells condoms, He's the only one in town,
Jesus He sells condoms, He's the only one in town,
Jesus He sells condoms, He's the only one in town,
Jesus saves, Jesus saves, Jesus saves.

Jesus can't play touch judge, cause His arms point both ways,
Jesus can't play touch judge, cause His arms point both ways,
Jesus can't play touch judge, cause His arms point both ways,
Jesus saves, Jesus saves, Jesus saves.

Jesus can't kick for touch, cause His feet are nailed together,

Jesus can't kick for touch, cause His feet are nailed together,
Jesus can't kick for touch, cause His feet are nailed together,
Jesus saves, Jesus saves, Jesus saves.

95. JINGLE BALLS

Dashing through the snow, almost in the nude,
Santa's bollocks glow, how nice to be so rude.
The bell at the whorehouse rings, he's reserved a cracking tart,
She always wears his foreskin down,
And at sixty-nine she don't fart.

Chorus:
Jingle balls, jingle balls, shag 'em all the way,
Oh what fun it is to ride on the eve of Christmas day, HEY,
Jingle balls, jingle balls, none of us are gay,
Oh what fun it is to shag on a one horse open sleigh.

Santa's on his way, his tunic's round his knees,
He's got his end away, and Rudolph ain't too pleased.
Up on the rooftop stood, rude thoughts his mind does dwell,
Starts playing with his pud, and some semen he does spill.
Chorus

The whore had squeezed him dry, Santa's got to go,
His foreskin she did fry, so he drags it in the snow.
Walks up to the sleigh, slips on a patch of come,
His legs are pulled away, he's got bruises on his bum.
Chorus

To Greenland he must go, to rest his mighty arse,
Children must now forgo, toys of which they've asked.
The moral is quite clear, while Santa's getting drunk,
To stop bruises on your rear, don't tread in reindeer spunk.
Chorus

96. JOHN BROWN'S PRICK

John Brown's prick was a fucking awful sight,
Mucked about with gonorrhoea and buggered up with shite,
The agonies of syphilis kept him awake all night,
But he still went rogering along.

 Chorus:
Oh the hoary old seducer
Oh the hoary old seducer
Oh the hoary old seducer
He still went rogering along

The colour of his water was a sort of orange-ade,
Little gonorrhoea germs within his scrotum played,
In spite of inconveniences, he went on undismayed,
Yes he still went rogering along.
 Chorus

Girls would come from miles around to his Baronial Hall,
To see his giant prick and his one remaining ball,
And see the rows of maidenheads all hung around the wall,
But he still went rogering along.
 Chorus

97. JOHN PEEL

Do you ken John Peel
With his balls of steel
And his prick of brass
And his celluloid arse,
Do you ken John Peel
With his balls of steel
And it all comes out in the morning.

98. JONESTOWN

(Sung to the tune of "Downtown")

CHORUS: You're in Jonestown - drinking with Reverend Jim.
Jonestown - chances are mighty slim.
Jonestown - people are dropping like flys.

When you're broke and your religion's a joke,
You can always go - to Jonestown
When life's incomplete only one man to meet,
Now won't you come and see - Jim Jones.

Watch him as he stirs the vat of Kool-aid that's so lethal.
Listen to the ani!uished cries of all the dying people.
No one survived.
The Reverend's a most gracious host,
So let's lift up our cups in the ultimate toast.

(CHORUS)

There was Congressman Ryan on his mission of spyin'
But he would not drink - with Jim Jones.
It was such a disgrace they had to blow off his face,
Now tell me who's to blame - Jim Jones.

Well this forced the Rev to put his final plan in action,
Then they drank the brew and saw with great satisfaction,
- Everyone died
Their deaths were both painful and slow,
But when to live is to die, there's only one way to go.
(CHORUS)
So the screams were a little loud - Jonestown.
Manson would sure be pround - Jonestown.
The Kool-Aid is waiting for you.

99. KATHUSALEM

In days of old there lived a maid,
She was the mistress of her trade,
A prostitute of high repute, the harlot of Jerusalem.

Chorus:
Hi Ho Kathusalem, Kathusalem, Kathusalem,
Hi Ho Kathusalem, the Harlot of Jerusalem.

It was a fact, she had a crack,
With hair so thick it could contract,
To fit the tool of any fool, who fucked in all Jerusalem.
Chorus

Now in a hovel by the wall, a student lived with but one ball,
Who'd shagged them all, or nearly all,
The harlots of Jerusalem.
Chorus

One night returning from a spree, his customary hard had he,
And on the street he chanced to meet,
The harlot of Jerusalem.
Chorus

He laid her down upon the grass,
Lifted her dress above her arse,
He grabbed his prick and made a pass,
At the fuck-hole of Jerusalem.
Chorus

But she was low and underslung,
He missed her twat and hit her bung,
Planted the seeds of many a son,
In the arse-hole of Jerusalem.
Chorus

Along came an Israelite, the bloody awful bastard shite,

He said he'd come to spend the night,
With the harlot of Jerusalem.
 Chorus

So when he saw the grunting pair,
With roars of rage he rent the air,
And vowed that he would soon take care,
Of the harlot of Jerusalem.
 Chorus

He seized the student by his crook,
And swearing on the Holy Book,
He flung him into Gabriel's brook,
That flows throughout Jerusalem.
 Chorus

Our hero rising from his plight,
Got the Israelite the bloody shite,
And stuffed him up with all his might,
The arse-hole of Kathusalem.
 Chorus

Kathusalem, she knew her part,
She spread her legs and blew a fart,
And blew the bastard all apart, right over old Jerusalem.
 Chorus

And buzzing like a bumble bee,
He caught his arse-hole on a tree,
Let that to you a warning be,
When passing through Jerusalem.
 Chorus

She gave birth to illigits, little shits with swinging tits,
Who sold their slits for threepenny bits,
The Harlots of Jerusalem.
 Chorus.

100. KNOBBY HALL

Oh his name was Knobby Hall, Knobby Hall,
Oh his name was Knobby Hall, Knobby Hall,
His name was Knobby Hall, and he only had one ball,
But it's better than none at all, fuck 'em all.

They say he stabbed his wife, stabbed his wife,
They say he stabbed his wife, stabbed his wife,
They say he stabbed his wife, but it wasn't with a knife,
No, it wasn't with a knife, fuck 'em all.
Oh the judge's name was Dick, name was Dick,
Oh the judge's name was Peck, name was Peck,
The judge's name was Peck, said,
"You killed her with your prick,
We shall stretch your fucking neck, fuck 'em all."

Oh the parson he come, he did come,
Oh the parson he come, he did come,
The parson he did come, with his tales of Kingdom Come,
He can shove them up his bum, fuck 'em all.

To the gallows he must go, he must go,
To the gallows he must go, he must go,
To the gallows he must go, and those buggers down below,
Think its all a bloody show, fuck 'em all.

He saw Lily in the crowd, in the crowd,
He saw Lily in the crowd, in the crowd,
He saw Lily in the crowd, and he hollered right out loud,
"Fuck you, Lily, ain't yer proud, fuck 'em all."

Well the hangman's name was Goose, name was Goose,
Well the hangman's name was Goose, name was Goose,
The hangman's name was Goose,
Had a cock so long and loose,
That he used it as a noose, fuck 'em all.

Now in heaven he does dwell, he does dwell,

Now in heaven he does dwell, he does dwell,
In heaven he does dwell, and he wasn't feeling well,
'Cause the whores are down in hell, Fuck 'EM ALL.

101. KNOCKERS

CHORUS:Oh, those knockers
Great big mama knockers
She's got a knocker here and a knocker over there
She's got a knocker here and a knocker there
And in between the knockers she's got a little hair
But oh, those knockers
Great big mama knockers
She's got a knocker here and a knocker over there

She's got a bra sized 39
You get inside it feels so fine

She's got a bra sized 56
You get inside and get your kicks

She's got a cunt like dynamite
When it explodes it still stays tight

She's got a bra sized 29
Titties are small but areolas are fine.

102. LET ME CALL YOU SWEETHEART

(Sung to the tune of "Let Me Call You Sweetheart")

Let me call you sweetheart,
I'm in love with you.
Let me rub your titties,
'Til they're black and blue.
Let me stroke your vulva,
'Til it's filled with goo.
Let's play hide the weeney,

Up your old wazoo.

103. LIFE PRESENTS A DISMAL PICTURE

Life presents a dismal picture
Dark and dreary as the womb,
Father's got an anal stricture
Mother's got a fallen womb.

Sister Sue has been aborted
For the forty-second time,
Brother Bill has been deported
For a homosexual crime.

Nurse has chronic menstruation,
Never laughs and never smiles,
Mine's a dismal occupation
Cracking ice for Grandpa's piles.

In a small brown paper parcel
Wrapped in a mysterious way
Is an imitation rectum
Granddad uses twice a day.

Joe the postman called this morning,
Stuck his prick through the door,
We could-not despite endearment
Get it out till half-past four.

Even now the baby's started
Having epileptic fits,
Every time it coughs it spews
Every time it farts it shits.

Yet we are not broken-hearted,
Neither are we up the spout,
Aunty Mabel has just farted,
Blown her arse hole inside out.

In the corner sits my sister,
Never laughs and never smiles.
What a dismal occupation:
Cracking ice for father's piles.

Brother Bill has been deported
For a homosexual crime.
Sister Sue has been aborted
For the sixth or seventh time.

Little Luke is slowly dying
For he's always having fits.
Everytime he laughs, he vomits;
Every time he farts, he shits.

104. LIL

Although a lady of ill-repute
Lilian Barker was a beaut,
And it was really deemed an honor
To be allowed to climb upon her.

Her lovely face was smooth and fair,
And golden was her flowing hair,
Yet pot and hash and cruel cocaine
Had ravaged heart and soul and brain.

Lil could take with sly content
A trooper or his regiment,
Hyperbole it sometimes seems,
Is not confined to wishful dreams.

But soon she had to see a doctor
To find out what disease had pocked her.
The diagnosis short and clear
Revealed a dose of gonorrhea.

As Lilian lay in her disgrace,
She felt the devil kiss her face,
She said, "Now mate I'm always willing
But first let's see your silver shilling."

105. LITTLE RED TRAIN

A little red train came down the track, she blew, she blew,
A little red train came down the track, she blew, she blew,
A little red train came down the track,
And I don't give a damn if she never comes back,
And she blew-oo-oo-oo-oo-oo-oo.

The engineer was at the throttle, she blew, she blew,
The engineer was at the throttle, she blew, she blew,
The engineer was at the throttle,
A-jacking off in a whisky bottle,
And she blew-oo-oo-oo-oo-oo-oo.

The fireman he was shovelling coal, she blew, she blew,
The fireman he was shovelling coal, she blew, she blew,
The fireman he was shovelling coal,
Right up the engineer's arsehole,
And she blew-oo-oo-oo-oo-oo-oo.

The switchman he was at the switch, she blew, she blew,
The switchman he was at the switch, she blew, she blew,
The switchman he was at the switch,
A-swishing away like a son of a bitch,
And she blew-oo-oo-oo-oo-oo-oo.

A blonde was in the dining car, she blew, she blew,
A blonde was in the dining car, she blew, she blew,
A blonde was in the dining car,
A-sucking away on a black cigar,
And she blew-oo-oo-oo-oo-oo-oo.

A porter was waiting in the car, she blew, she blew,
A porter was waiting in the car, she blew, she blew,

A porter was waiting in the car,
To take the place of the black cigar,
And she blew-oo-oo-oo-oo-oo-oo.

The flagman he stood out in the grass, she blew, she blew,
The flagman he stood out in the grass, she blew, she blew,
The flagman he stood out in the grass,
The staff of the flag run up his arse,
And she blew-oo-oo-oo-oo-oo-oo.

Hobo Bill was riding the rods, she blew, she blew,
Hobo Bill was riding the rods, she blew, she blew,
Hobo Bill was riding the rods,
When ninety nine cars rolled over his cods,
And she blew-oo-oo-oo-oo-oo-oo.

The railroad cop was in the yard, she blew, she blew,
The railroad cop was in the yard, she blew, she blew,
The railroad cop was in the yard,
Holding his billy and making it hard,
And she blew-oo-oo-oo-oo-oo-oo.

106. 65 LUPE

(Sung to the tune of "Red River Valley")

'Twas down in Cunt Valley where the red river flows,
Where cocksuckers flourish and maidenheads grow.
'Twas there I met Lupe the girl I adore,
She's my hot fucking, cocksucking Mexican whore.

She got her first piece at the ripe age of eight,
As she swung back and forth on the old garden gate.
The cross member broke and the upright ran in,
And she's lived ever since in a welter of sin.

She'll suck you, she'll fuck you, she'll gnaw on your nuts,
And if you're not careful she'll suck out your guts.
She'll wrap her legs round you 'til you think you'll die,

Oh I'd rather eat Lupe than sweet cherry pie.

Now Lupe is dead as she lies in her tomb,
As the maggots crawl into her decomposed womb.
The smile on her face seems to say "Give me more!"
She's my hot fucking, cocksucking Mexican whore.

107. LYDIA PINKHAM

CHORUS:So we'll drink, drink, drink to Lydia Pinkham,
The savior of the human race,
The human race.
Oh, she makes, she bottles, she sells the Vegetable
Compound,
And any man can sit on her face,
Sit on her face.

Now, Mr._____ had a very small penis,
He could barely make it stand,
Make it stand.
So we gave him the Vegetable Compound,
Now he come in either hand,
In either hand

Now Miss _____ had a very small bosom,
They scarcely showed beneath her blouse,
Beneath her blouse.
So we gave her the Vegetable Compound,
And now they milk her with the cows,
With the cows.

Now, Mr. _____ had very small testes,
They looked lik e a couple of peas,
Couple of peas.
So we gave him the Vegetable Compound,
Now they hang below his knees,
Below his knees.

108. MAGGIE MAY

CHORUS:Oh, my darling Maggie May
They have taken her away,
And no more down Lime Street will she roam
For the judge he guilty found her
For robbing a homeward bounder,
That dirty, robbin', no good Maggie May

I was a sailor bound for home,
All the way from Sierra Leone,
And two pound ten a month
Had been my pay,
As I jingled in my tin
I was sadly taken in
By the lady of the name of Maggie May.

When I steered into her
I just hadn't a care
I was cruisin' up and down
Ol' Canning Place.
'She was dressed in a gown so fine,
like a frigate of the line,
And I bein' a sailorman, gave chase.

She gave me a saucy nod,
And I like a farmer's clod
Let her take me line abreast in tow,
And under all plain sail
We ran before the gale
And to the Crow's Rest Tavern
We did go.

Next morning when I awoke,
I found that I was broke.
No trousers, coat or wallet could I find,
And when I asked her where
She said, "My dear young sir,
You'll find them in the pawnshop

Number nine."

To the pawnshop I did go,
No trousers could I find,
So the cops they came
And took this girl away.
Oh, you thieving Maggie May,
You robbed me of my pay,
It'll pay your fare out to Botany Bay.

She was chained and sent away
From Liverpool one day.
The lads they cheered
As she sailed down the bay,
An' every sailor lad
He only was too glad,
They'd sent the old tart to Botany Bay.

Oh Maggie, Maggie May,
They have taken you away,
To stay on Van Dieman's cruel shore.
Oh you robbed many a whaler
And many a drunken sailor,
But you'll never cruise
Round Liverpool no more.

109. MASTURBATION

Last night I laid awake and masturbated,
It felt so good, I knew it would.
Last night I laid awake and masturbated,
It felt so nice, I did it twice.

You should have seen me on the short strokes,
It felt so grand, I used my hand.
You should have seen me on the long strokes,
It felt so neat, I used my feet.

Slam it, ram it, throw it on the floor,

Wrap it around the bed post, slam in in the door.
Some people think that fornication is so neat,
But I would rather stay at home, and calmly beat my meat.
Eeeeeeeeee!

110. MEN

Men, men, men, men, men, men, men, men
Oh, it's great to be on a ship with men
We'll sail across the sea
Oh, we don't know where we'll land or when
But it's great to be with men
It's great to be with men.

'Cause men can sweat and men can stink
And no one seems to care
Oh, we'll throw the dishes in the sink
And clog the drain with hair-o
Clog the drain with hair-o.

Men, men, men!
On a ship all filled with men
We'll never have to lift the seat
There's no one here but men, men, men, men
Men, men, men, men.

We're men and friends until the end
 and none of us are sissies
At night we sleep in separate beds
And blow each other kissies
Blow each other kissies.

Men, men, men!
On a ship all filled with men
So batten down the ladies' room
There's no one here but men, men, men, men
Men, men, men, men.

Oh, there's men above and men below

And men down in the galley
There's Butch and Spike and Biff and Bill
And one that we call Sally
One that we call Sally.
Men, men, men!

On a ship all filled with men
So throw your rubbers overboard
There's no one here but men!
Ah Men!

111. MISS MILLY

Young Miss Milly was sweet and fair,
With snow white tits and curly hair,
Oh, unhappy maiden.
Her heart was happy, her step was light,
But she was a fool and one dark night

She got herself put in a pregnant plight
By a lecherous, lewd and
lustful cruel deceiver.

She went to this home but as she'd feared
The filthy old bastard had disappeared,
Oh, unhappy maiden.
Her mother declared: "Get out, you whore.
So never again dare to darken my door,
With your lecherous, lewd and
lustful cruel deceiver."

All night she wandered through the snow
How she suffered who can know,
Oh, unhappy maiden.
And when the morning cockerel cried,
Poor abandoned Milly had died
Frozen stiff as she lay outside.
Oh, the lecherous, lewd and
lustful cruel deceiver.

Hark all you young maidens,
the moral is clear
If you trust these foul bastards,
you'll shed many a tear
Like this oh, so unhappy maiden.
So bear this in mind: the semen may spill
And you'll find yourself getting more than your fill.
Precautions are best;
take a birth control pill
With your lecherous, lewd and
lustful cruel deceiver.

112. MONK OF GREAT RENOWN

There was an old monk of great renown,
There was an old monk of great renown,
There was an old monk of great renown,
Who fucked all the women around the town.

Chorus :
(spoken) The old sod, the dirty old sod,
 The bastard deserves to die.
(sung)   Glory glory hallelujah,
(spoken) Let us pray.
    A prayer for the constipated......SHIT
    A prayer for the frustrated.........FUCK
    A prayer for the menstruated....BLOODY HELL

He took a maid to the Abbot's bed, (3x)
And fucked and fucked her till she was dead.
 Chorus

His brother monks cried out in shame, (3x)
So her fucked her and fucked her to life again.
 Chorus

He met another by the mill, (3x)
And shagged her and shagged her up the hill.

Chorus

He met another in the hay, (3x)
And put her in the family way.
Chorus

His brother monks to stop his frolics, (3x)
Put a nail through his arse and cut off his bollocks.
Chorus

And now he's dead and in his box, (3x)
The dirty old bastard has got the pox.
Chorus

And now the moral I will tell,
And now the moral I will tell,
When all the world just feels like hell,
Just shag and shag till all is well.

113. MONTE CARLO

As she walked along the Bois de Boulogne
With a heart as heaavy as lead
She wishes that she was dead
She had lost her maidenhead
Her heart in a funk and covered with scorn
Her knickers were torn
and her cunt was worn
She's the girl that lowered the price
at Monte Carlo.

As he walked along the Bois de Boulogne
With his prick upon the stand
The girls all say it's grand
To take it in their hand
You give them a bob and they're on the job
Pulling the foreskin over the knob
Of the man who broke the bank
at Monte Carlo.

114. MRS. MURPHY

Give a cheer, give a cheer
For the men who drink the beer
In the cellar of Murphy's saloon.
They are brave, they are bold
And the stories that are told
In the cellar of Murphy's saloon.
For it's guzzle, guzzle, guzzle
As they pour it down their muzzle
And shout out their orders loud and clear:
"More beer."
For it's more, more, more
As the cops break down the door
In the cellar of Murphy's saloon.

Won't you put it in your mouth Mrs. Murphy,
For it only weighs a quarter of a pound,
It's got hair on its neck like a turkey
And it spits when you rub it up and down.

If I had the wings of an eagle
And the balls of a hairy baboon,
I'd fly up to the top of the mountain
And jack off on the man in the moon.

Now you say you're still a virgin
But you're cherry is not there anymore,
So why don't you quit trying to be so perfect
And do the thing that you're best known for.

For now you've got a throat like Linda Lovelace
And a cunt like the great cathouse whore,
So why don't you please do my pecker a favor
And deep throat me on the barroom floor.

Now we've got a team called _____,
And peckers as long as a broom,
So won't you please do your pussy a favor

And keep us mother fuckers out of your room.

We'll eat you, beat you, and mistreat you,
While we're singing our dirtiest verse,
Then we'll stick it in your ear and dick you from the rear,
For that's how we build up our thirst.

Sung by the whore house quartet.
Did you go and get it? Not yet.
Are you gonna get it? You bet.
Who you gonna get it from? Ginnette.

115. MY GOD HOW THE MONEY ROLLS IN

(Sung to the tune of "Bring Back My Bonnie")

CHORUS: Rolls in, rolls in,
My God how the money rolls in, rolls in,
Rolls in, rolls in,
My God how the money rolls in.

My father makes book on the corner,
My mother makes illicit gin,
My sister sells kisses to sailors,
My God how the money rolls in.

My cousin's a Harley Street surgeon,
With instruments long, sharp, and thin,
He only does one operation,
My God how the money rolls in.

My aunt keeps a girl's seminary,
Teaching young girls to begin,
She doesn't ask where they finish,
My God how the money rolls in.

Uncle Joe is a registered plumber,

His business is in holes and in tin,
He'll plug your hole for a tanner,
My God how the money rolls in.

My sister's a barmaid in Sydney,
For a shilling she strips to the skin,
She's stripping from mom to midnight,
My God how the money rolls in.

My brother's a poor missionary,
He saves fallen women from sin,
He'll save you a blonde for a guinea,
My God how the money rolls in.

My mother's a bawdy house keeper,
Every night when the evening grows dim,
She hangs out a little red lantern,
My God how the money rolls in.

My grandad sells cheap prophylactics,
And punctures them all with a pin,
For grandma gets rich from abortions,
My God How the money rolls in.

My uncle is carving out candles,
From wax that is surgically soft,
He hopes it'll fill up the gap,
If ever his business wears off.

I've lost all me cash on the horses,
I'm sick from the illicit gin,
I'm falling in love with my father,
My God what a mess I'm in.

116. MY GRANDFATHER'S COCK

My Grandfather's cock was too long for his jock,
So it dragged ninety yards on the floor,
It was bigger by far than the old man himself,

And it weighed not a pennyweight more.
With a horn on the morn of the day that he was born,
And a horn on the day that he died,
My Grandfather's cock was too long for his jock,
So it stood for his honour and pride.

117. MY OLD MAN

CHORUS:Sing a little bit,
Fuck a little bit.
Follow the band, toot, toot,
Follow the band with your cock in your hand.

My old man was a miner, a miner,
Worked all day in the pit.
Sometimes he'd shovel up coal dust,
And sometimes he'd shovel up shit.

My old man is a carpenter, a carpenter,
And a mighty fine carpenter is he.
All day long he screws screws in
And then he comes home screws me.

My old man is a taxidermist, taxidermist,
And a might fine taxidermist is he.
All day long he stuffs animals,
And then he comes home and stuffs me.

My old man is a trumpeter, a trumpeter,
And a very fine trumpeter is he.
All day long he blows trumpets,
And then he comes home and blows me.

118. NELLI 'AWKINS

Recite (Cockney accent)
I first met Nellie 'Awkins

down the Old Kent Road.
Her drawers were hanging down,
'Cos she'd been with Charlie Brown,
I pressed a filthy tenner
in her filthy 'rotton 'hand.
And that's how it all begun.

Sung

She wore no blouses
And I wore no trousers,
And she wore no underclothes,
And when she caressed me
She danm near undressed me
It's a thrill that no one knows.

I went to the doctor,
He said, "Where have you knocked her?"
I said, "Down where the green grass grows."
He said, quick as a twinkle,
"The Dimple on your dinkle
Will be bigger than a red, red rose."

I caught a dose of Pox a year ago
Year ago year ago
I thought it was the knot rot
And it would go
But the longer it lasted
The worse it grew
And now I've got the galloping grot rot
What shall I dooo

A year ago I lost my starboard ball
And now the other ones begun to fall
I'm rotting away
I'll be sorry some day
C'os then I'll have no balls at all.

My Rhubarb refuses to rise
To its Natural size

MARKET GARDENING size
My Rhubarb refuses to rise
Cos My Baby doesn't love me
My Baby doesn't love me
My Baby doesn't love me
No more or or!

119. NELLY CARTWRIGHT

CHORUS:Oh the moon shines down
on Nelly Cartwright,
She couldn't fart right,
her twat was airtight,
And though she tried
she couldn't start right,
With a knife she'd watched her
Promised Land.

Nell was a mountain maid
Who always was afraid,
That a drunken sot might fill her twat,
As she lay sleeping in the shade,
She took her fears in hand
and filled it up with sand
To keep the boys from stolen joys
In Nelly's Promised Land.

Now there was a trapper wise,
Who sought out Nelly's prize,
With a dead coyote on the end of his boot,
He made young Nelly open her eyes,
But as soon as she came to life
She reached for her hunting knife,
A flash in the air, a cry of despair,
And she severed his love life.

Oh women if you want to be wives
Put away those knives,
The men might pay for a lay in the hay,

But they're not gonna pay
for the rest of their lives,
My old mother said
if you're lying in your bed,
If you can't get aid, don't reach for a blade,
Have a bloody good fuck instead.

120. NO BALLS AT ALL

CHORUS:No balls at all, no balls at all,
She married a man who had no balls at all.

Come all you drunkards, give ear to my tale,
This short little story will make you turn pale,
It's about a young lady - so pretty and small,
Who married a man who had no balls at all.

How well she remembers the night they were wed,
She rolled back the sheets and crept into bed,
She felt for his prick, how strange, it was small,
She felt for his balls, he had no balls at all.

Mommy, oh mommy, oh pity my luck,
I've married a man who's unable to fuck,
His tool bag is empty, his screwdriver's small,
Tle impotent wretch has got no balls at all.

Daughter, my daughter, now don't be so sad,
I had the same trouble with your dear old pad,
There's many a man who'll come to the call,
Of the wife of the man who's got no balls at all.

The pretty young girl took her mother's advice,
And found the whole thing exceedingly nice,
An eleven pound baby wg bom in the fall,
To the wife of the man who has no balls at all.

The husband was joyous, got high as a kite,
The sight of that infant filled him with delight,

Though its head was too large, and its body too small,
The great thing about him - he had no balls at all.

121. NOW LISTEN A WHILE, AND I WILL TELL

Now listen a while, and I will tell,
Of the Gelding of the Devil of Hell;
And *Dick* the Baker of *Mansfield* Town,
To *Manchester* Market he was bound,
And under a Grove of Willows clear,
This *Baker* rid on with a merry Cheer:
Beneath the Willows there was a Hill,
And there he met the Devil of Hell.
Baker, quoth the Devil, tell me that,
How came thy Horse so fair and fat?
In troth, quoth the *Baker*, and by my fay,
Because his Stones were cut away:
For he that will have a Gelding free,
Both fair and lusty he must be:
Oh! quoth the Devil, and saist thou so,
Thou shalt geld me before thou dost go.
Go tie thy Horse unto a Tree,
And with thy Knife come and geld me;
The *Baker* had a Knife of Iron and Steel,
With which he gelded the Devil of Hell,
It was sharp pointed for the nonce,
Fit for to cut any manner of Stones:
The *Baker* being lighted from his Horse,
Cut the Devil's Stones from his Arse.
Oh! quoth the Devil, beshrow thy Heart,
Thou dost not feel how I do smart;
For gelding of me thou art not quit,
For I mean to geld thee this same Day seven-night.
The *Baker* hearing the Words he said,
Within his Heart was sore afraid,

He hied him to the next Market Town,
To sell his Bread both white and brown.
And when the Market was done that Day,
The *Baker* went home another way,
Unto his Wife he then did tell,
How he had gelded the Devil of Hell:
Nay, a wondrous Word I heard him say,
He would geld me the next Market Day;
Therefore Wife I stand in doubt,
I'd rather, quoth she, thy *Knaves Eyes* were out.
I'd rather thou should break thy Neck-bone
Than for to lose any manner of Stone,
For why, 'twill be a loathsome thing,
When every Woman shall call thee Gelding
Thus they continu'd both in Fear,
Until the next Market Day drew near;
Well, quoth the good Wife, well I wot,
Go fetch me thy Doublet and thy Coat.
Thy Hose, thy Shoon and Cap also,
And I like a Man to the Market will go;
Then up she got her all in hast,
With all her Bread upon her Beast:
And when she came to the Hill side,
There she saw two Devils abide,
A little Devil and another,
Lay playing under the Hill side together.
Oh! quoth the Devil, without any fain,
Yonder comes the Baker again;
Beest thou well *Baker*, or beest thou woe,
I mean to geld thee before thou dost go:
These were the Words the Woman did say,
Good Sir, I was gelded but Yesterday;
Oh! quoth the Devil, that I will see,
And he pluckt her Cloaths above her Knee.
And looking upwards from the Ground,
There he spied a grievous Wound:

Oh! (quoth the Devil) what might he be?
For he was not cunning that gelded thee,
For when he had cut away the Stones clean,
He should have sowed up the Hole again;
He called the little Devil to him anon,
And bid him look to that same Man.
Whilst he went into some private place,
To fetch some Salve in a little space;
The great Devil was gone but a little way,
But upon her Belly there crept a Flea:
The little Devil he soon espy'd that,
He up with his Paw and gave her a pat:
With that the Woman began to start,
And out she thrust a most horrible Fart.
Whoop! whoop! quoth the little Devil, come again I
pray,
For here's another hole broke, by my fay;
The great Devil he came running in hast,
Wherein his Heart was sore aghast:
Fough, quoth the Devil, thou art not sound,
Thou stinkest so sore above the Ground,
Thy Life Days sure cannot be long,
Thy Breath it fumes so wond'rous strong.
The Hole is cut so near the Bone,
There is no Salve can stick thereon,
And therefore, *Baker*, I stand in doubt,
That all thy Bowels will fall out;
Therefore *Baker*, hie thee away,
And in this place no longer stay.

122. OGGIE LAND

Half a pound of flour and rice, makes a lovely cracker,
Just enough for you and I, cor bugger janner,
Oh how happy us'll be, when us gets to the West Country,
Where the oggies grow on trees, cor bugger janner.

Where be that blackbird to, I know where he be,
He be up yon worzel tree, and I be after he.
Now he sees I, and I sees he, and he knows I be after he,
With a bloody great stick I'll hack 'ee down,
Blackbird I'll have 'ee.

Twenty five years I worked on this farm,
And you can't take the piss out of I,
And we'll all go down to oggie land,
To oggie land, to oggie land,
And we'll all go down to oggie land,
Where they can't tell the difference
Between tissue paper, tissue paper,
Marmalade and jam, Hey ! Milk with the hard on, ICE
CREAM !

123. OLD KING COLE

Old King Cole was a bugger for his hole,
And a bugger for his hole was he,
He called for his wife in the middle of the night,
And he called for his fiddlers three.
Now every fiddler had a fine fiddle,
And a very fine fiddle had he,
Fiddle diddle dee diddle dee, said the fiddlers,
Merry men are we,
There's none so fair as can compare as the boys from the
West Country.

Old King Cole was a bugger for his hole,
And a bugger for his hole was he,
He called for his wife in the middle of the night,
And he called for his tailors three.
Now every tailor had a fine needle,
And a very fine needle had he,
Stick it in and out, in and out, said the tailors,
Fiddle diddle dee diddle dee, said the fiddlers,
Merry men are we,

There's none so fair as can compare as the boys from the West Country.

Old King Cole was a bugger for his hole,
ŠAnd a bugger for his hole was he,
He called for his wife in the middle of the night,
And he called for his jugglers three.
Now every juggler had a fine ball, and very fine ball had he,
Throw your balls in the air, said the jugglers,
Stick it in and out, in and out, said the tailors,
Fiddle diddle dee diddle dee, said the fiddlers,
Merry men are we,
There's none so fair as can compare as the boys from the West Country.

Old King Cole was a bugger for his hole,
And a bugger for his hole was he,
He called for his wife in the middle of the night,
And he called for his butchers three.
Now every butcher had a fine chopper,
And very fine chopper had he,
Put it on the block, chop it off, said the butchers,
Throw your balls in the air, said the jugglers,
Stick it in and out, in and out, said the tailors,
Fiddle diddle dee diddle dee, said the fiddlers,
Merry men are we,
There's none so fair as can compare as the boys from the West Country.

Old King Cole was a bugger for his hole,
And a bugger for his hole was he,
He called for his wife in the middle of the night,
And he called for his horsemen three.
Now every horseman had a fine saddle,
And very fine saddle had he,
Ride it up and down, up and down, said the horsemen,
Put it on the block, chop it off, said the butchers,
Throw your balls in the air, said the jugglers,
Stick it in and out, in and out, said the tailors,

Fiddle diddle dee diddle dee, said the fiddlers,
Merry men are we,
There's none so fair as can compare as the boys from the
West Country.

Old King Cole was a bugger for his hole,
And a bugger for his hole was he,
He called for his wife in the middle of the night,
And he called for his huntsmen three.
Now every huntsman had a fine horn,
And very fine horn had he,
Wake up in the morn with a horn, said the huntsmen,
Ride it up and down, up and down, said the horsemen,
Put it on the block, chop it off, said the butchers,
Throw your balls in the air, said the jugglers,
Stick it in and out, in and out, said the tailors,
Fiddle diddle dee diddle dee, said the fiddlers,
Merry men are we,
There's none so fair as can compare as the boys from the
West Country.

Old King Cole was a bugger for his hole,
And a bugger for his hole was he,
He called for his wife in the middle of the night,
And he called for his coalmen three.
Now every coalman had a fine sack,
And very fine sack had he,
Want it in the front or the back, said the coalmen,
Wake up in the morn with a horn, said the huntsmen,
Ride it up and down, up and down, said the horsemen,
Put it on the block, chop it off, said the butchers,
Throw your balls in the air, said the jugglers,
Stick it in and out, in and out, said the tailors,
Fiddle diddle dee diddle dee, said the fiddlers,
Merry men are we,
There's none so fair as can compare as the boys from the
West Country.
Old King Cole was a bugger for his hole,
And a bugger for his hole was he,

He called for his wife in the middle of the night,
And he called for his policemen three.
Now every policeman had a fine beat,
And very fine beat had he,
I got the beat, got the beat, said the policemen,
Want it in the front or the back, said the coalmen,
Wake up in the morn with a horn, said the huntsmen,
Ride it up and down, up and down, said the horsemen,
Put it on the block, chop it off, said the butchers,
Throw your balls in the air, said the jugglers,
Stick it in and out, in and out, said the tailors,
Fiddle diddle dee diddle dee, said the fiddlers,
Merry men are we,
There's none so fair as can compare as the boys from the
West Country.

124. OLD KING COLE WAS A MERRY SOLE

Old King Cole was a merry old soul,
And a merry old soul was he.
He called for his wife in the middle of the night,
And he called for his fiddlers three.
Now every <u>fiddler</u> had a very fine <u>fiddle</u>,
And a very fine <u>fiddle</u> had he.
<u>Fiddle diddle de diddle de said the fiddler,</u>
What merry men are we.
There's none so fair as can compare with the boys of the
(your team) RFC.

Replace underlined words with the following words for other verses:

Jugglers
Juggler --Balls
Balls
Toss your Balls in the air, in the air said the jugglers

Barmaids
Barmaid -- Cunt
Cunt
Pull it out, pull it out said the barmaids

Cyclists
Cyclist -- Cycle
Cycle
Round and round said the cyclists

Flutists
Flutist --Flute
Flute
Root-diddly-oot-diddly-oot, said the flutists

Tailors
Tailor --Needle
Needle
Push it in and out, in and out said the tailor

Horsemen
Horseman -- Horse
Horse
Wop it up and down, up and down said the horsemen

Carpenters
Carpenter --Hammer
Hammer
Bang away, bang away said the carpenters

Coalmen
Coalmen -- Shovel
Shovel
Do you want it in the front, or the back said the coalmen

Surgeons
Surgeon --Scalpel
Scalpel
Cut it around the knob, and make it throb said the surgeons

Butchers
Butcher --Cleaver
Cleaver
Put it on the block and chop it off said the butchers

Parsons
Parson -- Shroud
Shroud
"Goodness gracious me!" said the parsons

Fishermen
Fisherman --Fish
Fish
Minus six feet long said the fishermen

Huntsmen
Huntsman --Bow
Bow
Up with the horn, in the morn said the huntsmen

125. ONCE THERE WAS A SERVANT GIRL WHOSE NAME WAS MARY JANE

CHORUS:Singing bell-bottom trousers,
coats of navy blue
Let him climb the rigging
like his Daddy used to do.

Once there was a servant girl
whose name was Mary Jane,
Her mistress she was good to her
She knew she was a country girl,
just lately from the farm,
And so she did her bloody best
to keep the girl from harm.

The forty-second Army Corps

came in to paint the town,
A band of bawdy bastards
and rapists of renown,
They busted every maidenhead,
and staggered out again,
But they never made the servant girl
who lived in Drury Lane.

Next there came the Fusiliers,
and a band of Welsh Hussars
They piled into the brothels,
they packed into the bars.
The maidens and the matrons
were seduced with might and main,
But they never made the servant girl
whose name was Mary Jane.

Early in the morning
when the sailor'd had his grind
He gave to her a ten bob note
to pacify his mind
Saying: "If you have a daughter
bounce her on your knee,
If you have a son
send the bastard out to sea."

Early one evening a sailor came to tea
And that was the start of all her misery,
At sea without a woman
for forty months or more,
There wasn't any need to
ask what he was looking for.

He asked her for a candle
to light his way to bed,
He asked her for a pillow
to rest his weary head,
Then using very gentle words,
as if he meant no harm

He asked the maid to come to bed
just to keep him warm.

She lifted up the covers
just a moment there to lie,
But he's got his dick inside her
before she could bat an eye,
And though he'd got her maidenhead
she showed no great alarm,
And the only words she said to him were:
"I hope you're keeping warm."

Now all you servant girls
take a warning from me,
Don't ever let a sailor
get an inch above the knee,
She trusted one, the ninny,
in his Naval uniform,
Now all she wants to do, me boys,
is keep the Navy warm.

126. O'REILLY'S DAUGHTER

CHORUS:Hi yi yi - Hi yi, yi, Hi yi yi,
The one-eyed Reilly.
Rub-it-up, shove-it-up, balls and all
Play it on your old base drum.

ALTERNATE
CHORUS:Yi-di-l-ay, Yi-di-l-oh,
Yi-di-l-ay for the one-eyed Reilly.
Rub-it-up, shove-it-up, balls and all
Jig-a-jig. Tres bon.

Jack O'Flannagan is my name,
I'm the king of copulation,
Drinking beer my claim to fame,
Shagging women my occupation.

Walking through the town one day,
Who should I meet but O'Reilly's daughter,
Not a word to her did say
But don't you think we really oughter.

Sitting one night in O'Reilly's bar
Drinking beer that was just like water,
Suddenly a thought ran through my head
I'd never tucked O'Reilly's daughter.

I took her gently by the hand
Led her upstairs like a lamb to slaughter,
Laid her gently on the bed
And quickly cocked my left leg over.

I tucked and tucked her on the bed,
Shagged and shagged until I stove her,
Having lost her maidenhead
She laughed like hell when the fun was over.

I fucked her standing
I fucked her lying,
If she'd had wings
I'd have fucked her flying.

I fucked her till her tits were flat,
Filled her up with soapy water,
She won't get away with that, if she doesn't
Have twins then she really oughter.

I heard footsteps on the stairs,
Old Man Reilly bent on slaughter,
With two pistols in his hand
Looking for the man who fucked his daughter.
I grabbed O'Reilly by the hair,
Stuck his bead in a bucket of water,
Rammed his pistols up his arse,
Damned quicker than I shagged his daughter.

Come you virgins, maidens fair,
Answer me quick and true no slyly,
Do you want it fair and straight and square,
Or the way I give it to the one-eyed Reilly.

Now I'm growing old and grey
And my tool is growing shorter,
But until my dying day
I'll remember O'Reilly's daughter.

127. POOR LITTLE ANGELINE

She was sweet sixteen on the village green,
Pure and innocent was Angeline,
A virgin still, never known a thrill
Poor little Angeline.

At the village fair the Squire was there
Masturbating on the village square
When he chanced to see the dainty knee
Of poor little Angeline.

Now the village squire had but one desire
To be the biggest fucker
in the whole damn shire,
He had set his heart on the vital part
Of poor little Angeline.

As she lifted up her skirt
to avoid the dirt
She slipped in a puddle
of the Squire's last squirt,
At the sight he saw,
how his dick grew raw
For poor little Angeline.

So he raised his hat and said:
"Miss, your cat

Has been run over and is squashed quite flat
Now my car is in the square
and I'll take you there
Oh poor little Angeline."

Now the filthy old turd
should have got the bird
But she climbed right in with a word,
As they drove away you could hear them:
"Poor little Angeline."

They had not gone far
when he stopped the car
And took little Angeline into a bar,
Where he gave her gin just to make her sin
Poor little Angeline.

When he'd oiled her well
he took her to a dell
There to give her bloody tucking hell,
And he tried his luck with a low down fuck
On poor little Angeline.

With a cry of "Rape" he raised his cape,
Poor little Angeline had no escape,
Now it's time someone came
to save the name
Of poor little Angeline.

Now the village blacksmith was brave and bold
And had loved little Angeline
for years untold,
And he vowed he'd be true
whatever they'd do
To poor little Angeline.

But sad to say that very same day
The blacksmith had gone to jail to stay
For cuming in his pants at the local dance

With poor little Angeline.

Now the window of his cell
overlooked the dell
Where the squire was giving
little Angeline hell,
And there on the grass he observed the fuck
Of poor little Angeline.

Now he got such a start that he let out a fart
And blew the whole bloody jail apart,
And he ran like shit
lest the Squire should split
His poor little Angeline.

When he got to the spot
and he saw what was what
He tied the villain's balls
in a granny knot,
For there upon the grass
was the imprint of the arse
Of poor little Angeline.

"Oh, blacksmith true, I love you, I do,
And I can tell by your trousers
that you love me too,
Here I am undressed,
come and do your best,
Cried poor little Angeline.

Now it would be wrong here
to end this song
For the blacksmith had a prick
fully one foot long,
And his natural charm
was as thick as your arm
Lucky little Angeline.

128. PUBIC HAIR

(Sung to the tune of "Baby Face")

Pubic hair, you've got the cutest little
Pubic hair
Nothing in the world can compare
To your pubic hair
Penis or vagina, nothing could be finer.

Pubic hair, I'm in heaven when I'm in your underwear
I didn't need a shove, I took a mouthful of
Your delicious pubic hair.

A vagina for your breakfast, a vagina for your lunch
A vagina for your dinner.
A vagina, munch, munch, munch!

So take a tip from Tom
And never eat your mom
A vagina can't be beat.

129. PUT ON YOUR BUSTLE

Put on your old bustle
And get out and hustle
For tomorrow the rent man is due.
Put your cunt in clever
With another loaded level
Don't return without a quid or two.

Put on your old suspenders
And get to mixing up the genders
There isn't any risk anyway.
The stud's been altered
And the bull's been haltered
In that good old fashioned way.

Put on your old pink panties

The ones that were your auntie's
Let's have a shageree in the hay.
While they're working in the field
We'll see what the crop can yield
In that good old fashioned way.

Put on your old grey corset
If it don't fit force it
For the army is moving in today.
As the bee makes honey
Let your cunt make money
In that good old fashioned way.

Put on the old green ointment
The fleas disappointment
And kill the buggers where they lay.
How it tickles and itches
It'll kill the sons-of-bitches
In that good old fashioned way.

130. QUEEN OF ALL THE FAIRIES

CHORUS:Twenty-one, never been done,
Queen of all the fairies.

Oh, she was a cripple with only one nipple
To feed the baby on.
Poor little tucker, he'd only one sucker
To start his life upon.

Ain't it a pity she'd only one titty
To feed tie baby on.
Poor little bugger, he'll never play rugger,
Nor grow up big and strong.

And as he got older and bolder and bolder,
And took himself in hand,
And flipped and flipped and flipped and flipped,
To the tune of an army band.

They tried him in the infantry,
They tried him on the land and sea,
The poor little bugger had no success,
He left everything in a terrible mess.

We see no hope for him unless
He joins the W.R.A.F.

131. RAJAH OF ASTRAKAN

The was a Rajah of Astrakan, Yo-ho, Yo-ho,
A most licentious cunt of a man, Yo-ho, Yo-ho,
Of wives he had one hundred and nine,
Including his favourite concubine,
Yo-ho, yer buggers, Yo-ho, yer buggers, Yo-ho, Yo-ho, Yo-ho.

One day when he had a hell of a stand, Yo-ho, Yo-ho,
He called to a warrior, one of his band, Yo-ho, Yo-ho,
"Go down to my harem, you lazy swine,
And fetch my favourite concubine,"
Yo-ho, yer buggers, Yo-ho, yer buggers, Yo-ho, Yo-ho, Yo-ho.

The warrior fetched the concubine, Yo-ho, Yo-ho,
A figure like Venus, a face divine, Yo-ho, Yo-ho,
The Rajah gave a significant grunt,
And parked his prick right up her cunt,
Yo-ho, yer buggers, Yo-ho, yer buggers, Yo-ho, Yo-ho, Yo-ho.

The Rajah bellowed loud and long, Yo-ho, Yo-ho,
The maiden's cries were short and strong, Yo-ho, Yo-ho,
But just when the ride had come to a head,
They both fell through the fucking bed,

Yo-ho, yer buggers, Yo-ho, yer buggers, Yo-ho, Yo-ho, Yo-ho.

They hit the floor with a hell of a crack, Yo-ho, Yo-ho,
Which completely ruined the poor girl's twat, Yo-ho, Yo-ho,
And as for the Rajah's magnificent cock,
It split down the middle because of the shock,
Yo-ho, yer buggers, Yo-ho, yer buggers, Yo-ho, Yo-ho, Yo-ho.

There is a moral to this tale, Yo-ho, Yo-ho,
There is a moral to this tale, Yo-ho, Yo-ho,
If you would try a girl at all,
Stick her right up against the wall,
Yo-ho, yer buggers, Yo-ho, yer buggers, Yo-ho, Yo-ho, Yo-ho.

132. RED FLAG

CHORUS: The working class can kiss my ass,
I've got the foreman's job at last.
The proletariat can kiss my fundamental orifice;
I'm upper class and off the dole,
So shove that red flag up your hole.

'Twas on Gibraltar's rock so fair
I saw a maiden lying there,
And as she lay in sweet repose,
A nasty wind blew off her clothes.

A sailor who was passing by
Removed his cap and winked his eye,
But as he saw to his despair,
She had the red flag flying there.

133. RHODEAN SCHOOL

CHORUS: Up school, up school, up school,
                          Tra La-la, La-la, La-la, La-la,
                          Tra La-la, La-la, La-la, La-la,

We are from Rhodean, Rhodean girls are we,
We take no pride in our virginity,
We take precautions, and avoid-abortions,
For we are from Rhodean School.

Our school doctor, she is a beaut,
Teaches us to swerve when our boyfriends shoot,
It saves many marriages, and forces miscarriages,
We are from Rhodean School.

We go to Rhodean, don't we have pluck,
We go to bed without asking a buck,
Try us sometime boys, you may be in luck,
We are from Rhodean School.

Our school gardener he makes us drool,
He's got a great big whopping, dirty tool,
All right for tunnels, and Queen Mary funnels,
And for the girls of Rhodean School.

We have a new girl, her name is Flo,
Nobody thought that she could have a go,
But she surprised the Vicar, by raising him quicker,
Than any other girl at Rhodean School.

We go to Rhodean, we can be had,
Don't take our word, boy, ask your old dad,
He brings his friends for breath-taking trends,
We are from Rhodean School.

Our house mistress you cannot beat,
She lets us go out walking the street,
We sell out titties for threepenny bitties,

We are from Rhodean School.

Our head mistress, her name is Jane,
She only likes it now and again,
And again, and again, and again,
We are from Rhodean School.

Our sport mistress she is the best,
Teaches us to develop our chest,
So we wear tight sweaters, and carry French letters,
We are from Rhodean School.

Our teacher Porter, he is a fool,
He's only got a teeny weeny tool,
It's only good for key holes, and little girlie's peeholes,
But not much for Rhodean School.

We go to Rhodean, don't we have fun,
We know exactly how it is done,
When we lie down we hole it in one,
We are from Rhodean School.

When we go down to the sea for a swim,
The people remark on the size of our quim,
You can bet your bottom dollar, it's as big as a horse collar,
We are from Rhodean School.

These girls from Cheltenham, they are just sissies,
They get worked up over one or two kisses,
It takes wax candles, and long broom handles,
To rouse the bowels of the girls from Rhodean School.

When we are invited to a dance,
We don't wear bras and we don't wear pants,
We like to give our boyfriends a chance,
We are from Rhodean School.

When we go down to the vicar's for tea,
He always lets us sit on his knee,

We make him randy and he gives us candy,
We are from Rhodean School.

134. RING A RANG A ROO

I had a girl in New Orleans, she was so young just sixteen,
She had blond hair and blue eyes too,
And she had a ring-a-rang-a-roo.

Chorus : Oh the ring-a-rang-a-roo,
Pray what is that ?
It's soft and warm like a pussy cat,
With hair all round and split in two,
That's what they call the ring-a-rang-a-roo.

She took me down into her cellar,
And said that I was a mighty fine fella,
She fed me wine and whiskey too,
And let me play with her ring-a-rang-a-roo.
Chorus

She took me up into her bed,
And placed a pillow beneath my head,
Took out my cock-a-doodle-doo,
And stuck it in her ring-a-rang-a-roo.
Chorus

Her mother said, "You bloody fool,
Because you've broke the golden rule,
So pack your bags and suitcase too,
And go and sell your ring-a-rang-a-roo.
Chorus

She went to town to become a whore,
She placed a sign above the door,
"One dollar each and three for two,
To take a crack at my ring-a-rang-a-roo."
Chorus

They came by two's, they came by four's,
Until at last they came in scores,
But she was glad when they were through,
For they had ruined her ring-a-rang-a- roo.
 Chorus

Now along came Pete, the son of a bitch,
He had blue balls & the seven year itch,
He had the pox and syphallis too,
And gave them all to the ring-a-rang-a-roo.
 Chorus

The army came, the army went,
The price went down to 50 cents,
They got the clap and syphilis too,
All for the love of her ring-a-rang-a-roo.
 Chorus

And now she's dead and buried deep,
Her body lies in Regent Street,
Her tits hang on the city wall,
And her pussy floats in alcohol.
 Chorus

135. RING THE BELL VERGER

CHORUS:Ring the bell, verger,
Ring the bell, ring,
Perhaps the congregation
Will condescend to sing.
Perhaps the village organist,
Sitting on his stool,
Will play upon his organ,
And not upon his tool.

Down in the belfry chauffeur lies,
Vicar's wife between his thighs.
Voice from pulpit from afar,
"Stop fucking wife and start fucking car."

Verger in the belfry stood,
Grasped in his hand, his mighty pud.
From afar the vicar yells,
"Stop pulling pud and pull fucking bells."

Ocean liner six days late,
Stoker stoking stoker's mate,
Voice from Captain o'er the wire,
'Stop fucking mate, start fucking fire."

136. RIP MY KNICKERS AWAY

CHORUS:Rip my knickers away,
Rip my knickers away,
I don't care what becomes of me,
As long as you finger my C-U-N-T.
Rip my knickers away, away,
Rip my knickers away,
Down the front, down the back,
Round the cunt, round the crack,
Rip my knickers away.

Be I Berkshire, be I buggery,
Oi koms up from Wareham,
Oi knows a gal with calico drawers,
And I knows how to tear 'em.

Walkin' by the field one day
I heard a maiden crying,
"Oh, please don't rip me knickers off, Jack,
You'll get there by and byin'."

137. ROLL ME OVER IN THE CLOVER
(Sung to the tune of "In The Clover")

CHORUS:Roll me over in the clover,
Roll me over, lay me down and do it again.

This is number one and the fun has just begun.

Oh, this is number two and my head is on her shoe.

Oh, this is number three and my hand is on her knee.

Oh, this is number four and we're grinding on the floor.

Oh, this is number five and I'm ready to muff dive.

Oh, this is number six and she said, "I love your tricks."

Oh, this is number seven and we're in tucking heaven.

Oh, this is number eight and the nurse is at the gate.

Oh, this is number nine and the quints are doing fine.

Oh, this is number ten and we're at it once again.

138. ROLL YOUR LEG OVER

CHORUS:O, roll your leg over
O, roll your leg over
O, roll your leg over
It's better that way.

I wish all little girls were like fish in a pool,
And I were a shark with a waterproof tool.

I wish all little girls were like chocolate sundays,
And I were a spoon I would dip in their undies.

I wish all little girls were like fish in the ocean,
And I were a whale so I could show them the motion.

I wish all little girls were like bricks in a pile,
And I were a mason so I could lay them in style.

I wish all little girls were like mares in the stable,
And I were a stallion so I could show them I'm able.

I wish all little girls were like cows in the pasture,
And I were a bull so I could fill them with rapture.

I wish all little girls were like fish in the brookie,
And I were a trout so I could get me some nookie.

I wish all little girls were like winds on the sea,
And I were a sail so I could have them blow me.

I wish all little girls were like B-29's,
And I were a jet so I could buzz their behinds.

I wish all little girls were like trees in the forest,
And I were a woodsman so I could split their clitoris.

I wish all little girls were like diamonds and rubies,
And I were a jeweler so I could polish their boobies.

I wish all little girls were like coals in the stoker,
And I were a fireman so I could shove in my poker.

I wish all little girls were like statues of Venus,
And I were the man with the petrified penis.

I wish all little girls were like little white rabbits,
And I were a hare to teach them bad habits.

I wish all little girls were like telephone poles,
And I were a squirrel to stuff nuts in their holes.

I wish all little girls were like little red foxes,
And I were a hunter so I could shoot up their boxes.
I wish all little girls were like bats in a steeple,

And I were a bat so there'd be more bats than people.

I wish all little girls were like bells in a tower,
And I were a clapper to bang by the hour.

I wish all little girls were like pieces of pie,
And I were a fork so I would fork till I die.

I wish all little girls were like small desert cactus,
And I were a pin, I would prick theirs for practice.

We sing long, we sing loud, we sing all about it,
But only because we've been doing without it.

139. ROLLER, ROLLER

Roller, Roller, Roller, Roller
Roller, Roller, Roller, Roller
Roll a silver dollar down upon the ground
And it will roll, because it's round
A woman doesn't know what a good man she's got
Until she turns him down, down, down, down
Listen my honey, listen to me
I want you to understand
As a silver dollar goes from hand to hand
A woman goes from man to man

A man without a woman is like a ship without a sail
Or a boat with a rudder
A fish without a tail
A man without a woman is like a wreck upon the sand
There's only one thing worse in the universe
And that's a woman (a what?)
I said a woman with a man

AB, AB, AB my boy
What are you waiting for now
You promised to marry me some day in June

It's never too late and it's never too soon
Oh! All the family keeps on asking me
Which way, what way, I'm in the family way
AB, AB, AB my boy
What are you waiting for now

I'm gonna wait til the sun shines Nellie
As the clouds go drifting by
We'll be so happy Nellie in the sweet by and by
Down Lover's Lane we'll wander
Sweethearts you and I
I'm gonna wait til the sun shines Nellie
In the sweet by and by

I don't want to go home, I don't want to go home
I'm in love with a beautiful girl
Down in the sewer shovelling manure
Listen to the turds go Clap! Clap! Clap!

140. ROYAL MARINE

In the depths of deepest Africa
Where no one's ever been
lies the body of an elephant
Shagged to death by the Royal Marines.
Royal Marines.
Royal Marines.
Shagged to death by the Royal Marines.

In the depths of deepest Antarctica
Where no one dares to go
Lies the body of a polar bear
Shagged to death by an Eskimo (Bambam).
Eskimo (Bambam).
Eskimo (Bambam).
Shagged to death by an Eskimo (Bambam).

141. RUGBY ALMA MATER

(Sung to the tune of "Alma Mater")

The rugby boys are out on the piss again,
Out on the piss again, out on the piss again.
The rugby boys are out on the piss again,
We want to wee-wee now - what do we want, boys.
We want to wee-wee now, we want to wee-wee now.
The rugby boys are out on the piss again,
We want to wee-wee now.

The rugger huggers want to much of fucky fucky,
Too much of fucky fucky, too much of fucky fucky.
The rugger huggers want too much of fucky fucky.
We want to wee-wee now, we want to wee-wee now.
The rugby boys are out on the piss again,
We want to wee-wee now.

142. RUGBY SONG

If I were the marrying kind,
Which thank the Lord I'm not, sir,
The kind of man that I would wed,
Would be a rugby hooker,

He'd hook balls, I'd hook balls,
We'd both hook balls together,
We'd be alright in the middle of the night
Hooking balls together.

If I were the marrying kind,
Which thank the Lord I'm not, sir,
The kind of man that I would wed,
Would be a rugby second row,

He'd push hard, I'd push hard,
We'd both push hard together,
We'd be alright in the middle of the night

Pushing hard together.

If I were the marrying kind,
Which thank the Lord I'm not, sir,
The kind of man that I would wed,
Would be a rugby lock.

He'd bind tight, I'd bind tight,
We'd both bind tight together,
We'd be alright in the middle of the night
Binding tight together.

If I were the marrying kind,
Which thank the Lord I'm not, sir,
The kind of man that I would wed,
Would be a rugby scrum half.

He'd put it in, I'd put it in,
We'd both put it in together,
We'd be alright in the middle of the night
Putting it in together.

If I were the marrying kind,
ŠWhich thank the Lord I'm not, sir,
The kind of man that I would wed,
Would be a rugby stand off.

He'd open up, I'd open up,
We'd both open up together,
We'd be alright in the middle of the night
Opening up together.

If I were the marrying kind,
Which thank the Lord I'm not, sir,
The kind of man that I would wed,
Would be a rugby centre.

He'd go straight, I'd go straight,
We'd both go straight together,

We'd be alright in the middle of the night
Going straight together.

If I were the marrying kind,
Which thank the Lord I'm not, sir,
The kind of man that I would wed,
Would be a rugby wing.

He'd go fast, I'd go fast,
We'd both go fast together,
We'd be alright in the middle of the night
Going fast together.

If I were the marrying kind,
Which thank the Lord I'm not, sir,
The kind of man that I would wed,
Would be a rugby full back.

He'd kick hard, I'd kick hard,
We'd both kick hard together,
We'd be alright in the middle of the night
Kicking hard together.

If I were the marrying kind,
Which thank the Lord I'm not, sir,
The kind of man that I would wed,
Would be a rugby referee.

He'd blow hard, I'd blow hard,
We'd both blow hard together,
We'd be alright in the middle of the night
Blowing hard together.

If I were the marrying kind,
Which thank the Lord I'm not, sir,
The kind of man that I would wed,
Would be a rugby spectator.

He'd come again, I'd come again,

We'd both come again together,
We'd be alright in the middle of the night
Coming again together.

143. RULE BRITANNIA

(Sung to the tune of "Rule Britannia")

Rule Britannia marmalade and jam,
Three firecrackers up your arse hole.
Bang! Bang! Bang!

Rule Britannia marmalade and jam,
Five Chinese firecrackers up your arse hole.
Bang! Bang! Bang! Bang! Bang!

Rule Britannia marmalade and jam,
Five thousand firecrackers up your arse hole.
Whoosh!!!

144. SAILOR BOY

All the nice girls love a candle,
All the nice girls love a wick,
For there's something about a candle
Which reminds them of a prick, prick, prick.
Nice and greasy, slips in easy,
Its a girlies pride and joy,
Its been up our Lady Jane,
And its going up again,
Ship Ahoy, Ship Ahoy.

145. SAMBO WAS A LAZY COON

Sambo was a lazy coon
Went to sleep in the afternoon
So tired was he

So tired was he
Into the jungle he did go
Swinging his copper to and fro
When along came a bee
A fucking great bumble bee.

Buzz, buzz, buzz, buzz, buzz,
Fuck off you bumble bee
I ain't no rose
I ain't syphillis tree
Get off my tucking nose
Get off my nasal organ
Don't you come near
If you want some honey
Better ask mummy cause you'll get no arsehole here.

Oh arsehole rules the navy
Arsehole rules the navy
Arsehold rules the navy but you'll get no arsehole here
Just beer, just beer, just beer, just beer.

146. SEVEN OLD LADIES

(Sung to the tune of "Oh Dear What Can The Matter Be")

Oh, dear, what can the matter be,
Seven old ladies locked in the lavatory,
They were there from Sunday to Saturday,
Nobody knew they were there.

They said they were going to have tea with the Vicar,
They went in together, they thought it was quicker,
But the lavatory door was a bit of a sticker,
And the Vicar had tea all alone.

The first was the wife of a deacon in Dover,
And though she was known as a bit of a rover,
She liked it so much she thought she'd stay over,
And nobody knew she was there.

The next old lady was old Mrs. Bickle,
She found herself in a desperate pickle,
Shut in a pay booth, she hadn't a nickel,
And nobody knew she was there.

The next was the Bishop of Chichester's daughter,
Who went in to pass some superfluous water,
She pulled on the chain and the rising tide caught her,
And nobody knew she was there.

The next old lady was Abigail Humphrey,
Who settled inside to make herself comfy,
And then she found out she could not get her bum free
And nobody knew she was there.

The next old lady was Elizabeth Spender,
Who was doing all right 'till a vagrant suspender
Got all twisted up in her feminine gender,
And nobody knew she was there.

The last was a lady named Jennifer Trim,
She only sat down on a personal whim
But she somehow got pinched twixt the cup and the brim,
And nobody knew she was there.

But another old lady was Mrs. McBligh,
Went in with a bottle to booze on the sly,
She jumped on the seat and fell in with a cry,
And nobody knew she was there.

147. SEVEN OLD FARTS
Missed song as a spacer

148. SHE WAS POOR

She was poor but she was honest,
Victim of a rich man's whim,

First he fucked her, then he left her, & she had a child by
him.

Chorus :
It's the same the whole world over,
It's the poor what gets the blame,
Its the rich that gets the pleasure,
Ain't it all a bleeding shame.

Then she came to London city,
Just to hide her bleeding shame,
But a Labour leader fucked her,
Put her on the streets again.
Chorus

See him riding in a carriage,
Past the gutter where she stands,
He has made a stylish marriage,
While she wrings her ringless hands.
Chorus

See him seated in his Rolls Royce,
Driving homeward from the hunt,
He's got riches from his marriage,
She's got corns upon her cunt.
Chorus

See her on the bridge at midnight,
Picking blackheads from her crutch,
She said, "Sir, I've never 'ad it."
I said, "No, not fucking much."
Chorus

See her stand in Piccadilly,
Offering her aching quim,
She is now completely ruined,
And it's all because of him.
Chorus

Then there came a wealthy pimp,
Marriage was the tale he told,
She had no one else to turn to,
So she sold her cunt for gold.
 Chorus

149. SHE WENT FOR A RIDE IN A MORGAN

She went for a drive in a Morgan,
She sat with the driver in front.
He fooled with her genital organs:
The more vulgar-minded say "cunt."

Now she had a figure ethereal,
She auctioned it out to men's cocks,
And contracted diseases venereal:
The more vulgar-minded say "pox."

The dazzling peak of perfection,
There wasn't a prick she would scorn,
She gave every man an erection:
The more vulgar-minded say "hom."

Did you ever see Anna make water?
It's a sight that you ought not to miss.
She can lead for a mile and a quarter:
The more vulgar-minded say "piss."

If I had two balls like a bison
And a prick like a big buffalo,
I would sit on the edge of creation
And piss on the buggers below.

150. SHOW ME THE WAY TO GO HOME

Show me the way to go home,
I'm tired and I wanna go to bed,

Well I had a little drink about an hour ago,
And its gone right to my head.
No matter where I roam, over land or sea or foam,
You will always hear me singing this song,
Show me the way to go home.

151. SING A SONG OF SYPHILIS

Sing a song of syphilis, a foreskin full of crabs,
Four and twenty blackheads, and a score or more of scabs.
And when the scabs were opened, the crabs began to sing.
And wasn't that a dirty thing to stick up Nellie's quim.

152. SING US ANOTHER ONE DO
(These are also know as Limericks)

CHORUS: That was a terrible song
So sing us another one
Just like the other one
So sing us another one do-oo

Alternate CHORUS:Aye, yi, Yi, Yi,
Your mother swims out to meet troop ships.
(Your mother does pushups on flagpoles.)
(They do it in China for chile.)
(They do it in Chile for china.)
(Your mother eats bat shit off cave walls.)
(Your mother thinks bedpans are soup bowls.)
(Your sister gives hand jobs on subways.)
(Your father gets cum in his mustache.)
(You brother beats off in confession.)
(Your father smells little girl's bicycle seats.)
(Your sister does squat-thrusts on fireplugs.)
(or any other distasteful verse you can think of)

So let's have another verse
That's worse than the other verse,
And waltz me around by my willy.

There once was a man from Rangoon,
Whose farts could be heard to the moon.
When you'd least expect 'em,
They'd explode from his rectum,
With the force of a raging typhoon.

The jolly old Bishop of Birmingham,
He buggered 3 maids while confirming 'em,
As they knelt seeking God,
He excited his rod,
And pumped his episcopal sperm in'em.

There once was a man named Skinner,
Who took a young lady to dinner,
At quarter past ten it was in her,
Dinner, not Skinner,
Skinner was in her before dinner.

There once was a man from Boston,
Who drove around in an Austin,
There was room for his ass,
And a gallon of gas,
But his balls hung out and he lost 'em.

Who swallowed a package of seeds,
Great tufts of grass,
Sprouted out of his ass,
And his balls were covered with weeds.

Aye, yi, yi, yi
Rodriguez, the Mexican pervert.
He ate out his mother
And cornholed his brother,
And waltzed me around by my willy.

There once was a lady from Peru,
Who filled her vagina with glue,
She said with a grin,

If they'll pay to get in,
They'll pay to get out of it too.

There was a couple named Kelly,
Who were stuck belly to belly,
Because of their haste,
They used library past,
Instead of petroleum jelly.

There was a young lady of Cheam,
Who crept into the vestry unseen,
She pulled down her knickers,
Likewise the vicar's,
And said, "How about it, old bean'?"

There once was a man from Racine,
Who built a big fucking machine,
Concave or convex,
It would fuck any sex,
Oh but what a bastard to clean.

There was a young German named Ringer
Who was screwing an opera singer,
Said he with a grin,
"Well, I've sure got it in!"
Said she, "It ain't your finger?"

There was a young lady named Hitchin,
Scratching her crotch in the kitchen,
Her mother said, "Rose,
It's the crabs I suppose?"
She said, "Yes and the buggers are itchin."

There was a young man of St. James,
Who indulged in the jolliest games,
He lighted the rim,
Of his grandmother's quim,
And made her piss through the flames.

There was a young woman named Wheeli
Who professed of no sexual feeling,
Until a cynic named Boris,
Nibbled at her clitoris,
Wheeling was scraped from the ceiling.

A hermit who had an oasis,
Thought it the best of all places,
He could pray and be calm,
'Neath a pleasant date palm,
While the lice on his penis ran races.

There was a young lady of Exeter,
So pretty, men craned their necks at her,
One went so far,
As to wave from his car,
The distinguishing mark of his sex at her.

There once was a man from Nantuckett,
With a cock so long he could suck it,
He said with a grin,
As he wiped off his chin,
"If my ear was a cunt I could fuck it."

Female apes were afraid of King Kong,
Since his wanger was exceedingly long,
Until a friendly giraffe,
Ate his yard and a half,
And ecstatically burst into song.

There was a young lady from Trent,
Who said she knew what it meant,
When he asked her to dine,
Private room, lots of wine,
She knew, she knew, but she went.

There once was a man from Madras,
Who balls were made from brass,
In windy Wea ther

They swung together,
And lightening shot out his ass.

In the Garden of Eden lay Adam,
Complacently stroking his madam,
For he knew in his mirth,
That on all of the earth,
There were only two balls and he had 'em.

A fellow whose surname was Hunt,
Trained his prick to do a stunt,
This versatile spout,
Could be turned inside out,
like a glove and be used as a cunt.

There once was a man from Kajowels,
Whose diet consisted of bowels,
When he couldn't get this,
He drank prostitute piss,
And scrapings from sanitary towels.

There was a woman from the Azores,
Whose body was covered with sores,
All the dogs in the street,
Would lick the green meat,
That hung down from her drawers.

That poor young fellow from Kent,
Whose cock was so exceedingly bent,
To save himself the trouble,
He ut it in double,
And instead of coming he went.

There once was a man named Bruno,
About tucking sheep he do know,
Lambs are fine,
And rams are divine,
But Lamas are numero uno.

There was a young lady named Hilda,
Who went for a walk with a builder,
He knew that he could,
And he should, and he would,
So he did, and he damn near killed her.

A young man with passions quite gingery,
Tore a hole in his Sister's best lingerie,
He slapped her behind,
And made up his mind,
To add incest to insult and injury.

There was a young lady of Crewe,
Whose cherry a chap had got through,
Which she told to her mother,
Who fixed her another,
Out of rubber, red ink, and glue.

When a lecherous priest at Leeds,
Was discovered, one day in the weeds,
Astride a young nun,
He said, "Christ this is fun,
Far better than fondling one's beads."

There was a young lady of Twickerham,
Who regretted men had no prick in 'em,
On her knees everyday,
To her God she would pray,
To lengthen, strengthen, and thicken 'em.

There was a young girl named McCall,
Whose cunt was exceedingly small,
But the size of her anus,
Was something quite heinous,
It could hold seven cocks and one ball.

There was a young parson named Binns,
Who talked about women and things,
But his secret desire,

Was a boy in the choir,
With a bottom like jelly on springs.

There was a young man of high station,
Who was found by a pious relation,
Making love in a ditch,
To I won't say a bitch,
But a woman of no reputation.

There was a young girl of Detroit,
Who at fucking was very adroit,
She could squeeze her vagina,
To a pinpoint or finer,
Or open it out like a quoit.

There was a young maid from Mobile,
Whose cunt was made of blue steel,
She got her thrills,
From pneumatic drills,
And off-centered emery wheels.

There was a young nun from Siberia,
Endowed with a virgin interior,
Until an old monk,
Jumped into her bunk,
And now she's the Mother Superior.

There was a young Scot from Delray,
Who buggered his father one day,
Saying, "I like it rather,
To stuff it up father,
He's clean and nothing's to pay."

There was a young plumber of Lea,
Who was plumbing a girl by the sea,
She said, "Stop your plumbing,
There's somebody coming!" -
Said he, still plumbing, "It's me."

There was an old man of Dundee,
Who came home as drunk as could be,
He wound up the clock,
With the end of his cock,
And buggered his wife with the key.

There was a young man from Lynn,
Whose cock was the size of a pin,
Said his girl with a laugh,
As she fondled his shaft,
"This won't be much of a sin."

An elderly pervert in Nice,
Who was long past wanting a piece,
Would jack-off his hogs,
His cows and his dogs,
Till his parrot called the police.

There was a young man from Cape Horn,
Who wished he had never been born,
And he wouldn't have been,
Had his father seen,
That the end of his rubber was torn.

The last time I dined with the King,
He did quite an unkingly thing,
While up on the throne,
He pulled out his bone,
And said, "If I play, will you sing?"

A comely young widow of Ransom,
Was ravished three times in a hansom,
When she cried out for more,
A voice from the floor,
Said, "Lady, I'm Simpson, not Sampson."

There once was a skater named Yeats,
Who attempted the splits while on skates,
But he fell on his cutlass,

Which rendered him nutless,
And now he is useless on dates.

From the depths of a crypt at St. Ciles,
Came a scream that resounded for miles,
Said the bishop, "Good gracious,
Has Father Ignatious
Forgotten the vicar has piles?"

There was an old Duke of Rockingham,
Who wrote a book on cunts and tucking 'em,
But a dirty old Turk,
Wrote a much better work,
On tits and 12 ways of sucking 'em.

There was a young girl from Yorkshire,
Who succumbed to her lover's desire,
She said, "Oh John, it's a sin,
But now that it's in,
Would you shove it a few inches higher?"

There was a young man from Brighton,
Who thought he had found a tight one,
He said, "Oh my love,
It fits like a glove."
She said, "But it's not in the right one."

There was a hermit from Behave,
Who kept a dead whore in his cave,
She only had one tit,
And smelled like shit,
But think of the money he saved.

There was a man of New Treaver,
Who had intercourse with a beaver,
The result of his screw,
Was a birchbark canoe,
Three ducks and an Irish retriever.

The gay young Duke of Buckingham,
Stood on the bridge at Rockingham,
Watching the stunts,
Of the cunts midst the grunts,
And all of the pricks fucking 'em.

There was a student of Trinity,
Who popped his sister's virginity,
Buggered his brother,
Had twins by his mother,
And took double honor in Divinity.

There once was a young Dr. Zuck,
In his ears her nipples got stuck,
With his thumb up her bum,
He could hear himself come,
Thus inventing the telephone tick.

The three old witches of Kent,
Took a man into a tent,
The three dirty bitches,
They pulled down his britches,
And jumped on his cock til it bent.

There was a young man named Pete,
Who was a bit indiscreet,
He pulled on his wong,
Until it grew very long,
And dragged down a two lane street.

There was a young man from Stroud,
Who was screwing a girl in a crowd,
A man up in front,
Said, "Hmmm, I smell cunt."
Just like that, not very loud.

There was a young lawyer named Springer,
Got his testicles caught in the wringer,
He hollered with pain

As they went down the drain,
"From now on I'll just use my finger."

Coitus upon a cadaver,
Is the ultimate way you can have 'er,
Her inanimate state,
Means a man needn't wait,
And eliminates all the palaver.

There once was a chick named Alice,
Who used a dynamite stick for a phallus,
When she got hot,
It finally went pop,
And they found her tits outside of Dallas.

There once was a girl from Nantuckett,
Who went to France in a bucket,
When she got there,
They asked for her fare,
She lifted up her dress and said fuck it.

I once knew a man named Magruder,
Who met a nude and he wooed her,
The nude thought it crude,
To be wooed in the nude,
But Magruder was shrewder and screwed her

There was a young girl from France,
Who jumped on a bus in a trance,
Six passengers fucked her,
Besides the conductor,
And the driver shot twice in his pants.

A pansy by the name of Bloom,
Took a lesbian up to his room,
They talked the whole night,
As to who had the right,
To do what, with which, and to whom.

There was a young man named Mirkin,
Who kept on jerkin' his gherkin,
Said his wife to Mirkin,
"Your duty you're shirkin',
That gherkin's for firkin', not jerkin'."

A young man whose sight was myopic,
Thought sex an incredible topic,
So poor were his eyes,
That despite its great size,
His prick appeared microscopic.

I once knew a girl named Delores,
Who had a six-inch clitoris,
While singing a chorus,
Her voice was so hoarse,
I checked her ID and it said Boris.

I once knew a man from LaGrange,
His mind was completely deranged,
In playgrounds he hung,
Looking at ten year old bun,
This was his home on the range.

There was a girl from Cape Cod,
Who thought babies were from God,
But 'twas not the Almighty,
Who hiked up her nightie,
'Twas Roger, the lodger, by God.

There once was a man named Hans,
Who planted an acre of cunts,
When in the fall,
They came up pubic hairs and all,
Hans ate cunts for months.

There was a young lady named Duff,
With a lively, luxuriant muff,
In his haste to get in her,

One eager beginner,
Lost both his balls in the rough.

There was a young man of Kildare,
Fucking a girl on the stairs,
The bannister broke,
But he doubled his stroke,
And finished her off in midair.

I once knew a man named Peese,
It was said he was quite a tease,
But along came Jan,
Who spread him some ham,
And together they made some cheese.

There was a young Turkish cadet,
And this is the damnedest one yet,
His tool was so long,
And incredibly strong,
He could bugger six Greeks en brochette

There was a dentist Malone,
Who fondled a girl patient alone,
But in his depravity,
He filled the wrong cavity,
And my how his practice has grown.

There once was a man named O'Dool,
Who had an enormous tool,
He'd use it to plow,
Or didle a cow,
Or as a cue stick at pool.

There once was a man from Shirue,
Who had warts all over his root,
He put acid on these,
And now when he pees,
He fingers his dick like a flute.

There was a soldier from Kildare,
Who fondled a girl in his chair,
At the sixty-third stroke,
The chair done broke,
And his gun went off in the air.

There was a young lady from Itching,
Sat scratching her crutch in the kitchen,
Her Mother said, ``Rose, it's pox I suppose,"
She said, ``Bollocks, get on with your knitting."

Chorus ;
 That was a beautiful song,
 Sing us another one,
 Just like the other one,
 Sing us another one do.

There was a young fella named Dave,
Who found a dead whore in a cave,
It took him some pluck to have a cold fuck,
But look at the money he saved.
 Chorus

There was a young girl from Australia,
Whose cunt did smell like a dahlia,
At 5p a smell it went very well,
At 10p a lick was a failure.
Chorus

There was a young girl from Cape Cod,
Who thought that all babes came from God,
It wasn't the Almighty who lifted her nighty,
It was Roger the lodger the sod.
 Chorus

There was a young lady from Gannon,
Who had an affair with the Reverend Buchanan,
She said with a grin, as he slipped it right in,
With those balls you should be a Cannon.

Chorus

There was a young man from Bengal,
Who had a hexagonal ball,
Its molecular weight was his prick times eight,
And twice the square root of fuck all.
 Chorus

There was a young maid from Mobile,
Whose cunt was made of blue steel,
She got her thrills from pneumatic drills,
And off-centred emery wheels.
 Chorus

There was a young nun from Siberia,
Endowed with a virgin interior,
Until an old monk jumped into her bunk,
And now she's the Mother Superior.
 Chorus

There was a young Scot from Delray,
Who buggered his father one day,
Saying I like it rather, to stuff it up father,
He's clean and there's nothing to pay.
 Chorus

There was a young plumber of Lea,
Who was plumbing a girl by the sea,
She said, ``Stop your plumbing, there's somebody coming.'
Said the Plumber still plumbing, ``It's me !''
 Chorus

The gay young Duke of Buckingham,
Stood on the bridge at Rockingham,
Watching the stunts of the cunts on the punts,
And the tricks of the pricks that were stuffing 'em.
 Chorus

There was a young girl from Azores,

Whose cunt was covered in sores,
All the dogs in the street, would lick the green meat,
That hung in festoons from her drawers.
 Chorus

There was a young sailor from Brighton,
Who remarked to his girl, "You're a tight one."
She replied, "Pon my soul, you're in the wrong hole,
There's plenty of room in the right one."

Chorus :
That was a funny old rhyme, here comes another verse,
Worse than the other verse, sing us another one do.

There was a young fellow named Charteris,
Put his hand where his young lady's garter is,
She said, "I don't mind, and up higher you'll find,
The place where my fucker and farter is."
Chorus

There were three ladies of Huxham,
And whenever we meets 'em, we fucks 'em,
And when that game grows stale, we sits on the rail,
And pulls out our pricks and they sucks 'em.
Chorus

There was a young man of Ostend,
Whose wife caught him fucking her friend,
"It's no use my duck, interrupting our fuck,
For I'm damned if I'll draw till I spend."
Chorus

There was a young German named Ringer,
Who was screwing an opera singer,
He said with a grin, "Well I've sure shoved it in!"
Said she, "You mean that ain't your finger."
Chorus

There once was a dentist named Stone,

Who saw all his patients alone,
In a fit of depravity, he filled the wrong cavity,
And my, how his practice has grown.
Chorus

A sailor who slept in the sun,
Woke to find his fly buttons undone,
He remarked with a smile, "Fuck me, a sundial,
And now it's a quarter to one."
Chorus

There was a young fellow of Harrow,
Whose john was the size of a marrow,
He said to his tart, "How's this for a start ?
My balls are outside in a barrow."
Chorus

There was a young lady named Mable,
Who liked to sprawl out on the table,
Then cry to her man, "Stuff in all you can,
Get your bollocks in to, if you're able."
Chorus

There was a young lass of Blackheath,
Who frigged an old man with her teeth,
She complained that he stunk, not so much from the spunk,
But his arsehole was just underneath.
Chorus

There was a young person of Kent,
Who was famous wherever he went,
All the way through a fuck, he would quack like a duck,
And he crowed like a cock when he spent.
Chorus

A parson who lived near Camborne,
Looked down on all women with scorn,
E'en a boy's fat, white bum, could not make him come,
But an old man's piles gave him the horn.

Chorus :
That was a rude old rhyme, sing us another verse,
Worse than the other verse, sing us another one do.

A mortician who practiced in Fife,
Made love to the corpse of his wife,
"How could I know, Judge, she was cold, did not budge,
Just the same as she'd acted in life."
Chorus

A Sultan of old Istanbul,
Had a varicose vein on his tool,
This evoked joyous grunts, from his harem of cunts,
But his boys suffered pain at the stool.
Chorus

There was an old man of Kentucky,
Said to his old woman, "Oi'll fuck 'ee."
She replied, "Now you wunt, come anigh my old cunt,
For your prick is all stinking and mucky."
Chorus

There was a young mate of a lugger,
Who took out a girl just to hug her,
"I've my monthlies," she said, "and a cold in the head,
But my bowels work well.....Do you bugger ?"
Chorus

There was a young man of Bengal,
Who went to a fancy dress ball,
Just for a stunt, he dressed up as a cunt,
And was fucked by a dog in the hall.
Chorus

There was a young man named McBride,
Who could fart whenever he tried,
In a contest he blew, two thousand and two,
Then shit and was disqualified.

Chorus

There was a young lady from Crewe,
Who filled her vagina with glue,
She said with a grin, "If they pay to get in,
They'll pay to get out of it too."
Chorus

A notorious whore named Miss Hearst,
In the weakness of men is well versed,
Reads the sign o'er the head, of her well rumpled bed,
"The customer always comes first."
Chorus

There was a young lady of Newcastle,
Who wrapped up a turd in a parcel,
And sent it to a relation, with this invitation,
"It has just come out hot from my arsehole."
Chorus

My old woman would wipe off her bum,
Of the clinkers that thereunto hung,
She would singe off the hair, that had sprouted down there,
And would lick her twat clean with her tongue.
Chorus

There was a young man of Jaipur,
Whose cock was shot off in the war,
So he painted the front to resemble a cunt,
And set himself up as a whore.

Chorus :
That was a jolly old rhyme, sing us another one,
Worse than the other one, sing us another one do.

There was an old girl of Silesia,
Who said, "As my cunt doesn't please ya,
You might as well come up my old slimy bum,
But be careful my tapeworm don't seize ya."

Chorus

There was a young man from Poole,
Who found a red ring round his tool,
He ran to the clinic, but the doctor, a cynic,
Said, "That's only lipstick, you fool."
Chorus

There was a young fellow named Bill,
Who took an atomic pill,
His navel corroded, his arsehole exploded,
And they found his burnt nuts in Brazil.
Chorus

There was a young man of Canute,
Who was troubled by warts on his root,
He put acid on these, and now when he pees,
He can finger his root like a flute.
Chorus

There was an old person of Gosham,
Who took out his bollocks to wash 'em,
His wife said, "Now Jack, if you don't put them back,
I'll step on your scrotum and squash 'em."
Chorus

Did you hear about young Henry Lockett ?
He was blown down the street by a rocket,
The force of the blast blew his balls up his arse,
And his pecker was found in his pocket.
Chorus

There was a young lady of Tring,
Who sat by the fire to sing,
A piece of charcoal, flew up her arsehole,
And burnt all the hair off her quim.
Chorus

There was a young man of Bombay,

Who fashioned a cunt out of clay,
But the heat of his prick, turned it into a brick,
And chafed all his foreskin away.
Chorus

A certain young fellow named Dick,
Liked to feel a girl's hand on his prick,
He taught them to fool, with his rigid old tool,
Till the cream shot out, white and thick.
Chorus

A bus-man named Abner McFuss,
Liked to suck off old men on his bus,
Then go out and sniff turds, and the arseholes of birds,
He sure was a funny old cuss.
Chorus

There was a young man named Morell,
Who played with his prick till he fell,
When to get up he started, he suddenly farted,
And fell down again from the smell.
Chorus

There once was a lady called Annie,
Who had fleas, lice and crabs up her fanny,
To get up her flue was like touring the zoo,
There were wild beasts in each nook and cranny.

Chorus :
That was a horrible rhyme,
Sing us another one, just like the other one,
Sing us another one do.

An insatiable nymph from Penzance,
Travelled by bus to south Hants,
Five others fucked her, besides the conductor,
And the driver came twice in his pants.
Chorus

There was a young man from Nantucket,
Whose cock was so long he could suck it,
He said with a grin as he wiped off his chin,
"If my ear was a cunt, I could fuck it."
Chorus

There was a young girl named McCall,
Whose cunt was exceedingly small,
But the size of her anus was something quite heinous,
It could hold seven pricks and one ball.
Chorus

There was a young man of St James,
Who indulged in the jolliest games,
He lighted the rim of his grandmother's quim,
And laughed as she pissed through the flames.
Chorus

There was a young man named Hentzel,
Who had a terrific long pencil,
He went through an actress, two sheets and a mattress,
And shattered the family utensil.
Chorus

There once was a rabbi named Keith,
Who circumcised men with his teeth,
It was not for the treasure, nor sexual pleasure,
But to get to the cheese underneath.
Chorus

There was a young man named Adair,
Who was fucking a girl on the stair,
The banister broke, and by doubling his stroke,
He finished her off in mid air.
Chorus

There was a young lady from Munich,
Who was ravished one night by a eunuch,
At the height of her passion he slipped her a ration,

From a squirt gun concealed in his tunic.
Chorus

A policeman from near Clapham junction,
Had a penis that just wouldn't function,
For the rest of his life he misled his wife,
With some snot on the end of his truncheon.
Chorus

Rudolph the red nosed reindeer,
Liked to stuff his stiff prick in his ear,
Christmas day he did come, and destroyed his eardrum,
And the spunk filled his left hemishere.

Chorus :
That was a fine Christmas rhyme, sing us another one,
Just like the other one, sing us another one do

Now the fairy at the top of the tree,
Exclaimed with a great deal of glee,
"This one branch up my cunt, is making me grunt, UGH!
But I've got room for another three."
Chorus

Now Santa we know is quite queer,
They say he likes it up the rear,
But he must be frustrated, should be castrated,
'Cos he only comes once a year.
Chorus

My tart put up the balloons,
It took her all afternoon,
Instead of blowing up the lot, she was blowing up my cock,
It reminded me of our honeymoon.
Chorus

She kissed me under the mistletoe,

It helped my flagging libido,
I stuck my hand down her drawers, she said,
"Oh, Santa Claus, have you a knob I can swallow ?"
Chorus

The fairies that pack Santa's toys,
When copulate make lots of noise,
It's a terrible din, As they play with their quim,
It's a pleasure they seem to enjoy.
Chorus

On a frosty Christmas day morn,
Santa arrived with a horn,
He said, "Bend over please, you may kneel on your knees,
Brr! I've got to park my cock somewhere warm."
Chorus

There was an old fellow called Santa,
Whose cock was stuck in a decanter,
They tried vaseline, and oxyacetyline,
Now the colour of his knob is magenta.
Chorus

Down the chimney pot old Santa slid,
On the fireplace he did skid,
Hit his head on the chair, sent his balls through the air,
And the smell of burnt pubics was acrid.
Chorus

Christmas dinner went with a swing,
Grandpa choked on a small bit of wing,
He said I feel quite a turd, cos I stuffed this dead bird,
And I burnt my knob cos its still roasting.
Chorus

153. SIR JASPER

She wears her silk pyjamas in the summer when its hot,
She wears a woollen nighty in the winter when its not,
But later in the Springtime and early in the Fall,

She jumps into bed with nothing on at all.

Chorus :
She's a most immoral lady,
She's a most immoral lady,
She's a most immoral lady,
As she lay between the sheets with nothing on at all
Oh Sir Jasper do not touch me ! (x3)
As she lay between the sheets with nothing on at all.

Oh Sir Jasper do not touch ! (x3)
As she lay between the sheets with nothing on at all.

Oh Sir Jasper do not ! (x3)
As she lay between the sheets with nothing on at all.

Oh Sir Jasper do ! (x3)
As she lay between the sheets with nothing on at all.

Oh Sir Jasper ! (x3)
As she lay between the sheets with nothing on at all.

Oh Sir ! (x3)
As she lay between the sheets with nothing on at all.

Oh ! (x3)
As she lay between the sheets with nothing on at all.

Glory, glory Hallelujah, see the devil coming to yer,
He's going to put his pitchfork through yer,
For jumping into bed with nothing on at all.

154. SIT ON MY FACE

(Sung to the tune of "Red River Valley")

On sit on my face and tell me that you love me.
I'll sit on your face and say I love you truly.
I love to hear you oralise,
When you're between my thighs,

You blow me away.

Sit on my face and let my lips embrace you.
I'll sit on your face until -you answer truly.
Life will be fine when we're both 69,
And we can sit on our faces in all kinds of places,
And wait 'til we're all blown away.

155. SOMBRERO

I-Yi-Yi-Yi, si, si, Senoira,
My sister Belinda just pissed out the window,
All over my brand new sombrero.

156. SOME DIE OF DRINKING WATER

Tune of British Grenadier

Some die of drinking water
And some of drinking beer.
Some die of constipation
And some of diarrhea
But of all the world's diseases
There's none that can compare
With the drip, drip, drip
Of a syphilitic prick
And they call it gonorrhea.

I like the girls who say they will,
I like the girls who won't.
I hate the girls who say they will
And then they say they won't.
But of all the girls I like the best
I may be wrong or right
Are the girls who say they never will
But look as though they might.

157. SOMETIMES I AM A TAPSTER NEW

Sometimes I am a Tapster new,
And skilful in my Trade Sir,
I fill my Pots most duly,
Without deceit or froth Sir:
A Spicket of two Handfuls long,
I use to Occupy Sir:
And when I set a Butt abroach,
Then shall no Beer run by Sir.
Sometimes I am a Butcher,
And then I feel fat Ware Sir;
And if the flank be fleshed well,
I take no farther care Sir:
But in I thrust my Slaughtering-Knife,
Up to the Haft with speed Sir;
For all that ever I can do,
I cannot make it bleed Sir.
Sometimes I am a Baker,
And Bake both white and brown Sir;
I have as fine a Wrigling-Pole,
As any is in all this Town Sir;
But if my Oven be over-hot,
I dare not thrust in it Sir;
For burning of my Wrigling-Pole,
My Skill's not worth a Pin Sir.
Sometimes I am a Glover,
And can do passing well Sir;
In dressing of a Doe-skin,
I know I do excel Sir:
But if by chance a Flaw I find,
In dressing of the Leather;
I straightway whip my Needle out,
And I tack 'em close together.

Sometimes I am a Cook,
And in *Fleet-Street* I do dwell Sir
At the sign of the Sugarloaf,
As it is known full well Sir:
And if a dainty Lass comes by
And wants a dainty bit Sir;
I take four Quarters in my Arms,
And put them on my Spit Sir.
In Weavering and in Fulling,
I have such passing Skill Sir;
And underneath my Weavering-Beam,
There stands a Fulling-Mill Sir:
To have good Wives displeasure
I would be very loath Sir;
The Water runs so near my Hand,
It over-thicks my Cloath Sir.
Sometimes I am a Shoe-maker,
And work with silly Bones Sir:
To make my Leather soft and moist,
I use a pair of Stones Sir:
My Lasts for and my lasting Sticks
Are fit for every size Sir
I know the length of Lasses Feet
By handling of their Thighs Sir.
The Tanner's Trade I practice,
Sometimes amongst the rest Sir;
Yet I could never get a Hair,
Of any Hide I dress'd Sir;
For I have been tanning of a Hide,
This long seven Years and more Sir;
And yet it is as hairy still,
As ever it was before Sir.
Sometimes I am a Taylor,
And work with Thread that's strong Sir
I have a fine great Needle,
About two handfulls long Sir.

The finest Sempster in this Town,
That works by line or leisure;
May use my Needle at a pinch.
And do themselves great Pleasure.

158. SONIA SNELL

This is the tale of Sonia Snell
To whom an accident befell,
An accident, as will be seen,
Embarrassing in the extreme.
It happened as it does to many
That Sonia went to spend a penny,
And entering with unconscious grace
The properly appointed Place,
There behind the railway station
She sat in silent meditation
Unfortunately unacquainted
The seat had recently been painted.
Too late did Sonia realize
Her inability to rise,
And though she struggled, pulled and yelled
She found that she was firmly held.
She raised her voice in mournful shout,
"Please, someone, come and get me out."
A crowd stood round and feebly sniggered,
A signalman said: "I'll be jiggered."
"Go blimey," said an ancient porter,
"We ought to soak her off with water."
The station master and his staff
Were most polite and did not laugh.
They tugged at Sonia's hands and feet
But could not shift her off the seat.
A carpenter arrived at last
And finding Sonia still stuck fast
Remarked: "I know what I can do."
And quickly sawed the seat in two.
Sonia arose, only to find

She'd a wooden halo on her behind,
But an ambulance drove down the street
And bore her off complete with seat.
They rushed the wood-bustled girl
Quickly into hospital
And grasping her hands and head.
Placed her face downwards on a bed.
The doctors came and cast their eyes
Upon the seat with some surprise.
A surgeon said: "Now mark my word
Could anything be more absurd?
Have any of you, I implore,
Seen anything like this before?"
"Yes," cried a student, unashamed,
"Frequently - but never framed."

159. STORMY WEATHER, BOYS

CHORUS:Stormy weather, boys,
stormy weather, boys,
When the wind blows
the barge will go.

We wanna sail but we're out of luck,
The skipper's dead drunk
in the Dog and Duck.

Skipper come aboard with a girl on his arm,
Come along me pretty missy.
there's no cause for alarm.

He said he liked her very, very much,
He asked her if she'd shag
and she kicked him in the crutch.

Skipper's dead drunk in the Dog and the Duck
Asking the barmaid if he can have a fuck.

Cook said he shouldn't be a skipper on a punt

We're all agreed he's a silly old cunt.

160. SUNSHINE MOUNTAIN

We're going up sunshine mountain,
Where the four winds blow.
We're going up sunshine mountain,
Faces all a-glow.
Turn your back on sorrow and hold your head high,
We're going up sunshine mountain,
You and I.

(Repeat about 500 times.)

161. SWEET VIOLETS

(Sung to the tune of "Sweet Violets")

CHORUS:Sweet violets,
Sweeter then all the roses,
Covered all over from arse to tit
Covered all over with shit.

Phyllis Quat she died in the springtime,
She expired in a terrible fit, -
We fulfilled her last dying wish, sir,
She was buried in six feet of -

Phyllis Quat kept a sack in the garden
I was curious I must admit,
One day I stuck in my finger
And pulled it out covered in -

Phyllis Quat took a bag to her boy friend's
But the bag was old and it split,
Now the boy friend and Phyllis have parted
For the bag was packed quite full of -

I sat on a gold lavatory

In the home of the Baron of Split,
The seat was encrusted with rubies
But as usual the bowl contained -

There was a professional tarter
Who could flatulate ballads and airs,
He could poop out the Moonlight Sonata
And accompany musical chairs, singing -

One day he attempted an opera
It was hard but the fool wouldn't quit,
With his head held aloft he suddenly coughed
And collapsed in a big heap of shit.

Well, now my song it is ended
And I have finished my bit
And if any of you feel offended
Stick your head in a bucket of shit.

162. SWING-LOW SWEET CHARIOT

(Sung to the tune of "Swing Low Sweet
Chariot")

Swing-low sweet chariot
Coming for to carry me home.
Swing-row sweet chariot
Coming for to carry me home.

I looked over Jordan
And what did I see
Coming for to carry me home
A band of angels coming after me
Coming for to carry me home.

If you get there before I do
Coming for to carry me home
Tell all my friends I'm coming too
Coming for to carry me home.

(Should be sung loudly and accompanied with pantomime, then whistled and accompanied
with pantomime, and then simply pantomimed without any other sounds.)

163. TAKE ME OUT FOR A GOOD BALL
(Sung to the tune of "Take Me Out To lle Ballgame")

Take me out for a good ball,
Lay me down on the ground.
Give me you penis and three stiff whacks,
If you come first, I won't ever come back.
For it's shoot, shoot, shoot for the hole please!
I can't believe you're so lame!
From the front, back, side, I don't care!
You're a damn bad lay!

164. TEAM CHANT
(Chanted)

We're a bunch of bastards,
Scum of the earth,
Filth of creation,
We're a bunch of masturbatin' sons of bitches,
Found in every whore house,
Drink, fight, and screw: mostly screw,
We of (insert your team name) RFC. say fuck you, FUCK
YOU.

(ALTERNATE)
(Shouted)

Cock suck, mother fuck, eat a bag of shit.
Asshole, douche bag, suck your mother's tit.
We're the best rugby team all the others suck.
(Insert your team name twice), yippee, yippee, fuck.

165. THE ALPHABET SONG

A is for Asshole all tattered and torn,
  CHORUS: Heigh Ho said Rolly.
B is the Bastard that's never been born,
  CHORUS: With a rolly polly, up 'em and stuff 'em,
Heigh Ho said Anthony Rolly.

Cis for Cunt all dripping with piss,
Dis the Drunkard who gave it a kiss.

Eis for Eunuch with only one ball,
Fis the Fucker with no balls at all.

Gis for Gonorrhea, Goiter, and Gout,
His the Harlot that spreads it about.

I is Injection for syphilis and itch,
J is the Jerk of a dog on a bitch.

K is for King who thought tucking a bore,
Lis the Lesbian who came back for more.

Mis for Maidenhead tattered and torn,
Nis the Noble who died with a horn.

Ois for Orifice now gently revealed,
Pis the Prick with the foreskin backpeeled.

Qis for the Quaker who shit in his hat,
Ris the Roger who rogered the cat.
·Sis for Shitpot, all full to the brim,
Tis the Turds that are floating within.

Uis for Usher who taught us at school,
Vis the Virgin who played with his tool.

W is for the Whore who made tucking a farce,

and X, Y, Z ... you can stuff up your arse.

166. THE BACHELOR'S SON

CHORUS:And when I die I'll surely fry
In the brimstone pots of hell,
But until that day,
And if you can pay,
Then I have sin to sell.

I'm a bachelor's son and I live in sin
With another man's wife at The Cross,
I've a fantan pool, a two-up school,
A brothel and a fourpenny doss.

I've three ex-wives running sly grog dives,
And my brother forges ten-pound notes,
For a union on the rocks
We can rig a ballot box,
With a million phoney votes.

I sell sex to moral wrecks
And drugs to damn your nerves,
Abortions, too, I can fix for you
We've a special line for perves.

Lesbian love and incest, too,
And flagellists quite a few,
And I've a special file
marked "Utterly Vile"
And an embalmed corpse
For a homo-necrophile.

167. THE CHASTITY BELT

O pray, gentle maiden,
let me be your lover,
Condemn me no longer

To mourn and to weep,
Struck down like a hart
I lie bleeding and panting
Let down your drawbridge
I'll enter your keep.
Enter your keep, nonny nonny,
Enter your keep, nonny nonny,
Let down your drawbridge,
I'll enter your keep.

Alas, gentle errant,
I am not a maiden,
I'm married to Sir Oswald,
The cunning old Celt,
He's gone to the wars
For a twelve month or longer
And taken the key
To my chastity belt.

Fear not, gentle maiden
For I know a locksmith.
To his forge we will go,
On his door we will knock
And try to avail us
Of his specialized knowledge
And see if he's able
To unpick your lock.

Alas, sir and madam,
To help I'm unable,
My technical knowledge
It is of no avail.
I can't find the secret
Of your combination
The cunning old Bastard
Has fitted a Yale.

I'm back from the wars
With sad news of disaster,

A terrible mishap
I have to confide,
As my ship was a-passing
The straits of Gibraltar
I carelessly dropped the key
Over the side.

Alas and alack, I am locked up forever
Then up stepped the page-boy me.
Saying leave this to me.
If you will allow me
To enter your chamber
I'll open it up with
My duplicate key.

168. THE CHURCH SONG - DING A DONG

On Sunday afternoon
While the church was turning out
The Vicar said to me,
"I bet I've been through
More women than you."
And the verger said, "You're on.
We'll stand by the gate
While the women pass by
And this shall be our sign
You ding Pong for the women you've had
And I'll ping pong for mine."

There were ding dongs
There were ping pongs
There were more ding dongs
Than there were more ping pongs
Till at last a woman went by
And the curate said, "Ding dong"
"Just a minute," said the Vicar,
"There's a mistake here
That is my wife I do declare."
"I don't give a bugger

I still been there
Ding a dong, ding a dong, ding a dong,
Ding Dong."

169. THE COUNTRY GENTLEMAN

CHORUS:Singing High Jig-a-Jig, Fuck a little pig.
Follow the band, Follow the band all the way.
Singing High Jig-a-Jig, Fuck a little pig.
Follow the band, Follow the band all the way.

I took my missus horse riding, horse riding
She stuck it as long as she could;
She stuck it and stuck it until she said, "Fuck it,
My arse hole is not made of wood."

I took my wife for a ramble, a ramble
Along a country lane.
She caught her-left tit on a bramble, a bramble
And arse over bollocks she came.

I asked her if it had hurt her, had hurt her
If she had gone through any pain.
Before she could answer, could answer,
She was arse over bollocks again.

170. THE ENGINEER

An engineer told me before he died,
 Chorus ;
 A Hum - Titty Bum, Titty Bum, Titty Bum,
 A Hum - Titty Bum, Titty Bum, Titty Bum.

An engineer told me before he died,
And I've no reason to believe he lied,
 Chorus

He had a wife with a cunt so wide,

Chorus
He had a wife with a cunt so wide,
That she could never be satisfied,
 Chorus

So he built a bloody great wheel,
 Chorus
So he built a bloody great wheel,
Two brass balls and a prick of steel,
 Chorus

The two brass balls he filled with cream,
 Chorus
The two brass balls he filled with cream,
And the whole bloody issue was driven by steam
 Chorus
He laid his wife upon the bed,
 Chorus
He laid his wife upon the bed,
And tied her legs behind her head,
 Chorus

He put the machine in a place to fuck,
 Chorus
He put the machine in a place to fuck,
He switched it on and wished her luck,
 Chorus

Round and round went the bloody great wheel,
 Chorus
Round and round went the bloody great wheel,
In and out went the prick of steel,
 Chorus

Up and down went the level of steam,
 Chorus
Up and down went the level of steam,
Down and down went the level of cream,
 Chorus

Now we come to the very sad bit,
 Chorus
Now we come to the very sad bit,
There was no way of stopping it,
 Chorus

She was split from cunt to tit,
 Chorus
She was split from cunt to tit,
And the whole fucking issue was covered in shit,
 Chorus

The moral of the story is,
 Chorus
The moral of the story is,
Always fit a safety switch.
Chorus

171. THE ERECTION FACTORY

(Sung to the tune of "Caissons Go Rolling Along")

CHORUS:Oh, it's Hi Hi Hee at the Erection Factory,
Shout out your orders loud and clear: HARD ON!
But it isn't too much fun when you know he just can't cum,
As he tries for the (first, second, etc.) time around.

You can tell at a glance that he doesn't stand a chance
As he tries for the first time around.
You can tell by his look that he needs to read a book
As he tries for the first time around.

You can tell by the size that he'll never get a rise
As he tries for the second time around.
You can tell by the feel that he's not a man of steel
As he tries for the second time around.

You can tell by his shape that he's not a good bedmate
As he tries for the third time around.

You can tell by his pud that he's really just a dud
As he tries for the third time around.

You can tell by the meat that it's gonna be a feat
As he tries for the fourth time around.
You can tell by his prick that it's gonna be a trick
As he tries for the fourth time around.

You can huff, he can puff, but he'll never get it up
As he tries for the fifth time around.
You can tell by his cock that you'd rather use a sock
As he tries for the fifth time around.

You can tell by his mauls that he hasn't got the balls
As he tries for the sixth time around.
You can tell by the fuck that you're gonna have to suck
As he tries for the sixth time around.

You can tell by the hump that he takes it in the rump
As he tries for the seventh time around.
You can tell by the sag that he really is a fag
As he tries for the seventh time around.

You can tell by his face that he can't keep up the pace
As he tries for the eighth time around.
You can tell it's too late and he'll never penetrate
As he tries for the eighth time around.

You can tell by his face that he's really lost in space
As he tries for the ninth time around.
You can tell by the groan that you've worn him to the bone
As he tries for the ninth time around.

You can tell by the whine that he can't go one more time
As he tries for the tenth time around.
You can tell it's too late and you'll have to masturbate
As he tries for the tenth time around.

He can masturbate for months but he'll only cum just once

As he tries for the eleventh time around.
You can tell by the blast that this time will be the last
As he tries for the eleventh time around.

You can tell he's a rugger cause he's such a damn good lover
As he makes it the last time around!

172. THE GANG BANG SONG

LEADER: Knock! Knock!
GROUP:Who's There?
LEADER:Orange.
GROUP:Orange who?
LEADER:Orange you glad we're going to have a gang bang
CHORUS:... and always Will,
Because a gang bang gives me such a thrill.
When I was younger and in my prime,
I used to gang bang all the time.
But now I'm older and turning grey,
I only gang bang once a day.

(Use this same basic format for other verses.)

Jewish.
Jewish who?
Jewish we had a gang bang...

Eisenhower.
Eisenhower who?
Eisenhower late for the gang bang...

Olive.
Olive who?
Olive a gang bang...

Lina.
Lina who?
Lina up against the wall, we're going to have a gang bang...

Santana.
Santana who?
Santana na na na na.........

Banana.
Banana who?
Banana na na na na.........

Orange.
Orange who?
Orange you glad I didn't say Santana na na na na ....

173. THE GOOD SHIP VENUS

CHORUS:Yo! Ho! Ho! We haven't got anymore beer.
There's frigging on the rigging;
Wanking on the planking,
Tossing on the crossing,
There was fuck all else to do.

Twas on the good ship Venus,
By God you should have seen us,
The figurehead was a whore in bed
And the mast the Captain's penis.

The captain of this lugger,
He was a dirty bugger,
He wasn't fit to shove shit
From one place to another.

The captain's wife was Mabel.
Whenever she was able,
She'd fornicate the second mate
Upon the galley table.

The ship's cook's name was Freeman,
My God was he a demon,
He fed the crew on menstrual stew

And hymens fried in semen.

The captain had a daughter,
Who fell into the water,
We heard her squeal and knew an eel
Had found her sexual quarter.

The first mate's name was Carter,
By God he was a farter,
When the high winds would cease
They's use Carter to start her.

The second mate's name was Andy,
His balls were long and bandy,
We filled his arse with molten brass
For wanking in the brandy.

The cabin boy was Kipper,
A dirty little nipper,
We stuffed his arse with broken glass
To circumcise the skipper.

The captain's name was Morgan,
By Christ he was a gorgon!
Ten times a day sweet tunes he's play.
On his productive organ.
The captain's daughter Mable,
They laid her on a table!
And all the crew would come and screw
As oft as they were able.

"Twas on a Chinese station,
We caused a great sensation.
We sunk a junk in a sea of spunk
By mutual masturbation.

The third mate's name was Paul,
He only had one ball.
But with cracker he rolled terbaccer

Around the cabin wall.

The captain's daughter Mary,
Had never lost her cherry.
The men grew bold and offered gold
And now there's no more Virgin Mary.

Another cook was O'Malley,
He didn't dilly dally.
He shot his bolt with such a jolt
He whitewashed half the galley.

The boatswain's name was Lester,
He was a hymen tester.
Thru hymens thick he stuck his prick
And left it there to fester.

Another one was Cropper,
Oh Christ he had a whopper.
Twice round the deck, around his neck
And up his bum for a stopper.

The ship's dog's name was Rover,
The whole crew had him over,
We ground that faithful hound
From Singapore to Dover.

The engineer was McTavish
And young girls he did ravish,
His missing dick's at Istanbul
He was a trifle lavish.

A homo was the Purser,
He couldn't have been worser,
With all the crew he had a screw,
Until they yelled: "Oh no sir."

So now we end this serial,
Through sheer lack of material.

I wish you luck and freedom from
Diseases venereal.

174. THE HAIRS ON HER DICKI DI DO

CHORUS:And the hairs on her dicki di do
Hang down to her knees.
One black one, one white one
And one with a little shite on,
And one with a little light on
To show us the way.

The Mayor of Bayswater
He has a lovely daughter.

If she were my daughter,
I'd have them cut shorter.

She lives on a cattle ranch,
And shits like a bloody avalanche.

On her first trip through Melbourne,
She strangled her firstborn.

I've smelt it and felt it,
It feels like a piece of velvet.

I've ate it and fucked it,
And even loose rucked it.

I've touched it and poked it,
And even rolled and smoked it.

It would take a coal miner,
To find her vagina.

She married an Italian,
With balls like a bloody stallion.

She divorced the Italian,
And married the stallion.

It's like going through a forest,
To find her clitoris.

I licked it, I pricked it,
I even fly hacked it.

Her love thought he had seduced her,
But it turned out he'd only goosed her.

One black one, one white one,
The white one was semen.

On a trip through Vladivostock,
She sampled a bit of horsecock.

She sits on a mountain,
And pisses like a bloody fountain.

One green one, one red one,
The red one she bled on.

It takes a _____ rugger,
To get down and FUCK HER.

175. THE HARLOT OF JERUSALEM

CHORUS: Hey, hey, Kathusalem, Kathusalem, Kathusalem
Hey, hey, Kathusalem,
The Harlot of Jerusalem.

In the land of King Knute,
There lived a girl of ill repute,
A lusty, busty prostitute,
The Harlot of Jerusalem.

The boys would come from miles around,
Just to ride her up and down,
She only charged a half a crown,
The Harlot of Jerusalem.

There came a man from Palestine,
My God, he was a Frankenstein,
He thought he'd have himself a time,
On the Harlot of Jerusalem.

He laid her on a shady nook,
And from his pants the bastard took,
A penis like a butcher's hook,
For the Harlot of Jerusalem.

As she spread her legs apart,
She did cut a mighty fart,
That shot them like a tucking dart,
O'er the walls of Jerusalem.

As he flew on out of sight
He did find to his delight,
The legs still wrapped around him tight,
Of the Harlot of Jerusalem.

As he flew so fancy free,
His balls did catch upon a tree,
And there they hang for all to see,
The shame of all Jerusalem.

176. THE HOLE IN THE ELEPHANT'S BOTTOM

I wanted to go on the stage
And now my ambition I've gotten,
In pantomime I'm all the rage
As the hole in the elephant's bottom.

His balls they hang so low

I think I could knot 'em,
As I wink at the girls in the pit
Through the hole in the elephant's bottom.

The man who plays the front part
Is absolutely rotten,
All he can do is to fart
Through the hole in the elephant's bottom.

One night we performed in a farce
And they stuffed up the bottom with cotton,
But it split and I showed my bare arse
Through the hole in the elephant's bottom.

There are pockets inside the cloth
For two bottles of Bass, if you've got 'em,
But they hiss and they boo when I blow out the froth
Through the hole in the elephant's bottom.

Now my part hasn't got any words
But there's nothing that can't be forgotten,
I spend all my time pushing property turds
Through the hole In the elephant's bottom.

Some may think that this story is good
And some may believe that it's rotten,
But those that don't like it can stuff it right up
The hole in the elephant's bottom.

177. THE KEYHOLE IN THE DOOR

CHORUS:Oh, the keyhole in the door, the door,
The keyhole in the door,
I took up my position by the keyhole in the door.

I was invited for the weekend
to a ball at Cholmondely Hall,
To celebrate the wedding
of Sue Vere and Cousin Paul.

I read the guest list over
and imagine my delight,
When I found Sweet Fanny Adams
had come to spend the night.

The ball was one of splendor,
all the city nobs were there,
Touching up the ladies
like farmers at the fair,
And Fanny fairly dazzled
as she danced around the floor,
I resolved lie in wait for her
by the keyhole in the door.

I left the ballroom early,
just after half-past nine,
And as I hoped to find it
her room lay next to mine,
So taking off my trousers
I set off to explore
And took up my position
by the keyhole in the door.

I hadn't long to wait there
wrapped in my dressing gown,
When I saw Fanny on the staircase,
retiring all alone,
She didn't lock her bedroom door
I couldn't ask for more,
And I crept out of the shadows
by the keyhole in the door.

First she removed her stockings,
her silken legs to show,
And then her frilly panties
to reveal her fur below,
"Now take off all the other things,"
was all I could implore,
And silently I gripped the knob

and crossed the threshold door.

Silently I shut the door
and took her in my arms,
And sooner than I'd expected,
discovered all her charms,
And in case another person
should see the sights I saw,
I hung her frilly panties
o'er the keyhole in the door.

The night I rode in glory
as I plumbed the girl's insides
And on her heaving belly
I had many splendid rides,
But when I woke next morning
my dick was red and sore,
And I felt that I'd been screwing
through the keyhole in the door.

178. THE KOTEX FACTORY

(Sung to the tune of "Caissons Go Rolling Along")

CHORUS: For it's Hi Hi Yee, in the Kotex Factory,
Shout out your sizes loud and clear.
Mumbo, Jumbo, Junior Miss, take it out when you piss.
For wherever you go, you will always know,
When the end of the month comes around.

You can tell from the stench that there's trouble in the
trench,
When the end of the month comes around.

You can tell from the stink that your cock will come out pink,
When the end of the month comes around.

When she asks you for a dime, you will know it's her
ragtime,
When the end of the month comes around.

When the sheets are all red, you will know it's time for head,
When the end of the month comes around.

You can tell from the smell, that tonight's gonna be hell,
When the end of the month comes around.

When she fondles in her purse, you will know she's got the
curse,
When the end of the month comes around.

When you see that little white string, you will know she's got
that thing,
When the end of the month comes around.

Pull that string, rip that cord, open up the old flood door,
RUN FOR COVER, IT'S A BLOODY GUSHER.

(ALTERNATE CHORUS AND VERSES.)

CHORUS: For it's high, high, hee in the Kotex factory,
               Shout out your orders loud and strong.
               Small! Medium! Large! Junior Miss! -Family
Size!
               Bale of Hay! Cotton Field!

You can tell by the rope that she's gonna tell you nope,
When the end of the month rolls around.

You can tell by the smell that there's trouble in the well,
When the end of the month rolls around.

You can tell by her walk that you're gonna sit and talk,
When the end of the month rolls around.

You can tell by the look that you shoulda read a book,
When the end of the month rolls around.

You can tell by her stance that you're only gonna dance,

When the end of the month rolls around.

You can tell by the lump that you're only gonna dry hump,
When the end of the month rolls around.

You can tell by the red that the best you'll get is head,
When the end of the month rolls around.

You can tell by the pad that you're not gonna be a dad,
When the end of the month rolls around.

You can tell by her legs that she's about to drop her eggs,
When the end of the month rolls around.

179. THE LOBSTER

CHORUS: Singing ho tiddly ho
                  Shit or bust!
                  Never let your bollocks dangle in the dust!

"Good morning Mister Fisherman."
"Good morning, Sir." said he.
"Have you a lobster you can sell to me?"

"Yes, Sir." said the Fisherman.
"I have two;
The biggest of the bastards I'll sell to you."

I took the lobster home
And I couldn't find a dish;
So I used the pot where the missus has a piss

In the middle of the night
The wife got out of bed;
She piddled in the pot on the lobster's head.

The missus gave a giggle
Then she gave a grunt;
A dirty big lobster hanging from her cunt.

The wife grabbed the shovel
And I grabbed the broom;
We chased that lobster round the room.

We hit it on the head,
We hit in on the side;
We hit it 'till the bloody lobster died.

The moral of this story
The moral, it is this:
Always have a look-see before you have a piss.
The Lobster (ALTERNATE VERSES.)

"Good morning, Mr. Fisherman."
"Good morning, Sir." said he.
"Have you a lobster you could sell to me?"

"Oh, yes Sir, yes Sir.
I have two;
The biggest of the bastards I will sell to yo

Well, I took the bastard home,
To give the wife a treat;
I put it in the piss pot to keep it sweet.

in the middle of the night,
As you might guess;
The wife got up to take herself a piss.

Well, first she gave a squeal,
And then she gave a grunt;
Because that tucking lobster bit her on the cunt.

Well, I grabbed a mop,
And the wife grabbed a broom;
We chased the lobster right around the room.

Well, we beat him on the back,

We beat him on the side,
We beat the lobster until the bastard died.

There's a moral to my story,
Which is simply this;
Always take a shufty before you take a piss.

This is the end of my story,
There isn't any more;
An apple's up my ass & you can eat the core.

180. THE LOBSTER SONG

Oh Mr Fisherman back from the sea,
Have you a lobster you can sell to me ?

 Chorus ;
 Singing roll tidly oh, shit or bust,
 Never let your bollocks dangle in the dust.

Yes sir, yes sir, I have two,
The biggest of the bastards I will sell to you.
 Chorus

We hit it on the head and we hit it on the side,
We hit the fucking lobster till the bastard died.
 Chorus

I took the lobster home, but I didn't have a dish,
So I put it in the place where the missus has a piss.
 Chorus

In the middle of the night, the missus arose,
Sat on the piss-pot and turned up her toes.
 Chorus

Up jumped the lobster with a smile on his kisser,
Reached up a claw and grabbed her on the pisser.
 Chorus

The missus said ``Fred,'' I said ``What ?''
She said ``Look, there's a lobster dangling from my twat !''
 Chorus

The missus grabbed a poker, and I grabbed the broom,
And we chased the fucking lobster round and round the
room.
 Chorus

We hit it on the head and we hit it on the side,
We hit the fucking lobster till the bastard died.
 Chorus

The moral of the story - the moral is this,
Always have a shufty before you have a piss.
 Chorus

That's the end of my story, there isn't anymore,
There's an apple up my arsehole - you can have the core.
 Chorus

Another end to my story, I don't give a fuck,
There's an orange up my arsehole - you can have a suck.
 Chorus

181. THE MAID OF THE MOUNTAIN GLEN

CHORUS: They called the bastard Stephen,
                They called the bastard Stephen,
                They called the bastard Stephen,
                For that was the name of the ink
                (Quink, Quink).

There was a maid of the mountain glen,
Seduced herself with a fountain pen.
The pen it broke and the ink ran wild,
And she gave birth to a blue-black child.

Stephen was a bonny child,
Pride and joy of his mother mild.
And all that worried her was this -
His steady stream of blue-black piss.

Mary of New Brighton Pier,
Seduced herself with a bottle of beer.
The top came off and the froth ran wild,
And she gave birth to a nut brown child.

FINAL
CHORUS: They called the bastard Frellfalls,
                 They called the bastard Frellfalls,
                 They called the bastard Frellfalls,
                 For that was the name of the beer
                 (Queer, Queer).

182. THE MAYOR OF BAYSWATER

The Mayor of Bayswater has got a pretty daughter,

Chorus:
And the hairs on her dicky-di-dow
hang down to her knees,
One black one, one white one,
And one with a little shite on,
And the hairs on her dicky-di-dow
hang down to her knees.

I've smelt it, I've felt it, its just like a bit of velvet,
Chorus

I've seen it, I've seen it, I've been right between it,
Chorus

She slept with a demon, who washed her with semen,
Chorus

She married an Italian with balls like a fucking stallion,
 Chorus

It would need a Coal-miner to find her vagina,
 Chorus

If she were my daughter, I'd have them cut shorter,

 And the hairs, on her dicky-di-dow,
 The hairs, on her dicky-di-dow,
 The hairs, on her dicky-di-dow,
 Hang down to her knees,
 Hang down, hang down, hang down, hang down,
 And the hairs on her dicky-di-dow,
 Hang down to her knees.

183. THE MINSTRELS SING OF A BASTARD KING OF MANY LONG YEARS AGO

CHORUS: He was forty, fat and full of fleas,
                 His scepter sat between his knees,
                 God bless the Bastard King of England.
The minstrels sing of a Bastard King
of many long years ago
Who ruled his land with an iron hand,
Though his mind was weak and low,
His only outer garment
was a dirty yellow shirt
With which he tried to hide his hide,
But he couldn't hide the dirt.

Now the Queen of Spain
was an amorous dame,
And a sprightly wench was she
And longed to play in a sexual way
With the King across the sea.

So she sent a secret message
With a secret messenger
To ask the King if he would string
Along to sleep with her.

Now Ol' Philip of France
he heard by chance
Within his royal court,
And he swore, "By God, she loves this slob
Because I'm rather short,"
So he sent the Duke of Suffering Sap
To give to the Queen a dose of clap
To pass it on to the
Bastard King of England.

When news of the foul deed was heard
Within fair London's walls
The King he swore by the Royal Whore
He'd have King Phillip's life.
He offered half the royal purse
And a piece of Princess Claire
To any British subject
Who'd undo Philip the Fair.

The Duke of Northerland saddled his horse
And galloped off to France,
He swore he was a fairy,
The King let drop his pants,
Then in front of a throng
He slipped on a thong
Leaped on his horse and galloped along
Dragging the Frenchman back
To Merrie Old England.

When the King of England saw the sight
He fell in a faint on the floor,
For during the ride his rival's hide
Was stretched a yard or more,
And all the whores in silken drawers

Came down to London town.

And should round the battlements,
"To Hell with the British Crown."
And Philip alone usurped the throne
His scepter was his royal bone,
With which he ditched
The Bastard King of England.

184. THE MOLE CATCHER

CHORUS: With his la ti lie diddle,
                   and his la ti lie day.
In Manchester city
by the sign of The Plough
There lived a mole catcher,
I can't tell you how,

He'd go out mole catching
from morning till night,
And a young fellow would
come for to visit his wife.

Now the mole catcher got jealous
of all the same thing,
And he hid under the wash house
to see what did come in.

Now this young fellow
comes climbing over the stile,
And the mole catcher's watching
with a crafty smile.

He knocks at the door
and this he does say,
"Where is your husband,
good woman, I pray?

"He's gone out mole catching,

you have nothing to fear."
Little did she know
the old bastard was near.

They went up the stairs
and she gives him the sign,
But the filthy old fellow
did creep up behind.

Now just as the young fellow
reached the height of his frolics,
The mole catcher grabs him
quite fast by the buttocks.

The trap it squeezed tighter,
the mole catcher did smile,
"Here's the best mole
we've caught in a while."

"I'll make you pay well
for ploughing me ground.
This little prank will cost you
all of ten pound."

"Oh," says the young fellow,
"Christ gov, I don't mind,
For it only works out
at tuppence a grind."

So come all you young fellows
and mind what you're at.
Don't ever get yours caught
in a mole catcher's trap.

185. THE MONK OF GREAT RENOWN

CHORUS: The old sod, the sod,
                The bugger deserved to die.

There was a monk of great renown,
Who shagged an innocent maid from town.

His brother monks they cried in shame,
So he turned her over and shagged her again.

He met another by the mill,
And shagged and shagged her up the hill.

He met another in the hay,
And put her in the family way.

He took her to the abbot's bed,
And shagged and shagged till she was dead.

But when the abbot cried, "Amen,"
He shagged her back to life again.

His brother monks to stop his mauls,
Put a nail through his dick and cut off his balls.

And now the moral I will tell,
And now the moral I will tell,

When all the world just feels like hell,
Just shag and shag till all is well.

186. THE NORTH ATLANTIC SQUADRON

CHORUS: Away, away with fife and drum
                  Here we come full of rum
                  Lookin' for women who'll peddle
                  their bum
                  On the North Atlantic Squadron
For forty days and forty nights
We sailed the broad Atlantic,
And never to pass a piece of arse,
It drove us nearly frantic.

The cock she ran around the deck
The Captain he pursued her,
He caught her on the afterdeck
The dirty bastard screwed her.

The cabin boy, the cabin boy,
The dirty little nipper,
He filled his bum with bubble gum,
And vulcanized the skipper.

The Captain loved the cabin boy,
He loved him like a brother,
And every night between the sheets
They cornholed one another.

The second mate did masturbate,
No dick was higher or wider
They cut off his dick upon a rock
For pissing in the cider.

In days of old when knights were bold,
And women weren't particular,
They lined them up against the wall
And fucked them perpendicular.

In days of old when men were bold,
And rubbers weren't invented,
They wrapped a sock around their cock
And babies were prevented.

We're off, we're off to Montreal,
We'll fuck the women, We'll fuck them all,
We'll pickle their cherries in alcohol,
On the North Atlantic Squadron.

There was a whore from Montreal,
She spread her legs from wall to wall,
But all she got was sweet fuck all

From the North Atlantic Squadron.

There was a whore from Singapore
Hung upside down inside a door,
And she was left split, worn and sore
By the North Atlantic Squadron.

187. THE PORTIONS OF THE FEMALE

The portions of the female
That appeal to man's depravity,
Are fashioned with considerable care,
And what at first appears
To be a modest cavity,
Is really as elaborate affair.
Now doctors who have studied
These feminine phenomena,
With numerous experiments on dames,
Have taken all the-items
Of the gentle sex's abdomina,
And given them all length Latin names.
There's the Vulva, the Vagina,
And of course the old Peronina,
And the Hymen that is often found in brides,
There's a lot of little things -
You'd love 'em if you see 'em,
The Clitoris and God knows what besides.
What a pity it is then,
That we common people chatter.
Of those mysteries to which I have referred,
And we use for such delicate
And complicated matter,
Such a very short and vulgar little word.
The erudite authorities who study
The geography
Of that obscure but entertaining land,
Are able to indulge a taste
For intricate topography,
And view the happy details close at hand.

But ordinary people though aware
Of their existence,
And complexities beneath the public know
Are normally content
Just to view them at a distance,
And treat them roughly speaking as a show.
And therefore when,
Probe the secrets of virginity,
Our methods are perhaps a little blunt,
We do not cloud the issue
With meticulous Latinity,
But call the whole concern a simple cunt.
For men have made this useful
And pleasure-giving article,
The topic of innumerable jibes,
And though the name is old
Which they have given to this particle,
It seems to fit the subject it describes.

188. THE PUPPY SONG

The puppies had a meeting, they came from near and far,
And some they came by aeroplane and some by motor car.
And when they were assembled according to the book,
Each puppy took his asshole and hung it on a hook.

The meeting was successful for puppy, bitch, and sire,
Till some grey spotted mongrel stood up and shouted fire.
The puppies they all panicked and without a second look,
Took any flaming asshole from any flaming hook.

The puppies were pathetic, their asses were so sore,
For each one had an asshole he'd never had before.
And that's the only reason a dog will leave a bone,
To sniff some doggy's asshole to see if it's his own.

189. THE RAJAH OF ASTRAKHAN

There once was a Rajah of Astrakhan, yo-ho, yo-ho,
The dirty old Rajah of Astrakhan, yo-ho, yo-ho,
He had more than one hundred wives, and twice as many
concubines,
Yo-ho you buggers, yo-ho you buggers, yo-ho, yo-ho, heave
ho.

He woke one night with a helluva stand, yo-ho, yo-ho,
And called the chief of his warrior band, yo-ho, yo-ho,
Go, my friendly warrior kind, and fetch my favorite
concubine,
Yo-ho you buggers, yo-ho you buggers, yo-ho, yo-ho, heave
ho.

He fetched his favorite concubine, yo-ho yo-ho,
Her face and her figure were both divine,, yo-ho, yo-ho,
But all the Rajah did was grunt and stuffed his tool right up
her cunt,
Yo-ho you buggers, yo-ho you buggers, yo-ho, yo-ho, heave
ho.

The Rajah was getting all heated and red, yo-ho, yo-ho,
The pace of his work had gone to his head, yo-ho, yo-ho,
But as the fuck was reaching a head, both poor buggers fell
out of bed,
Yo-ho you buggers, yo-ho you buggers, yo-ho, yo-ho, heave
ho.

They hit the floor with a helluva smack, yo-ho, yo-ho,
Which completely shattered the woman's crack, yo-ho, yo-
ho,
And as for the Rajah's once proud cock, it never withstood
the shock,
Yo-ho you buggers, yo-ho you buggers, yo-ho, yo-ho, heave
ho.

Now at night when the Rajah's in bed, yo-ho, yo-ho,

His once proud tool never raises its head, yo-ho, yo-ho,
All battered and bruised, and bent in the middle, it's all the
poor bugger can do to piddle,
Yo-ho you buggers, yo-ho you buggers, yo-ho, yo-ho, heave
ho.

As to most stories there's a moral to tell, yo-ho, yo-ho,
And, of course, there's a moral to this one as well, yo-ho, yo-
ho,
When screwing a pro, or a conc' or a whore, don't do it too
hard or you'll fall on the floor!
Yo-ho you buggers, yo-ho you buggers, yo-ho, yo-ho, heave
ho.

190. THE RAM OF DERBYSHIRE

CHORUS: If you don't believe me
              Or if you think I lie
              Go ask the girls of Derbyshire
              They'll tell you the same as 1.

There was a ram of Derbyshire
That had two horns of brass,
The one grew out of its head, sir,
The other grew out of its ass.

When the ram was young, sir,
It had a nasty trick
Of jumping over a five-barred gate
And landing on its prick.

When the ram was old, sir,
They put in a truck
And all the girls of Derbyshire
Came out to have a fuck.

When the ram was dead, sir,
They buried it in St. Paul's,

It took twelve men and a donkey cart
To carry away its balls.

191. THE RING DANG DOO

CHORUS: Now the Ring Dang Doo,
Pray, what is that?
So soft and round like a pussy cat,
So soft and round and split in two,
That's what they call the Ring Dang Doo.

I got a gal in New Orleans,
She's young, just sweet sixteen,
She's young, and pretty too,
And she's got what they call
The Ring Dang Doo.

She took me down into her cellar,
She said I was a very fine feller,
She fed me with wine, and whiskey too,
And she let me play
With her Ring Dang Doo.

She took me up into her bed,
Placed a pillow beneath my head,
Took out my dick a doodle -- doo,
And stuck it in
Her Ring Dang Doo.

Now her mother said, "You goddamn fool,
You have broken the golden rule,
So pack your bags and your suitcase too,
And go to hell with
Your Ring Dang Doo."

Now she went to town to become a whore,
She placed a sign upon her door,
"Two dollars down, the rest I'll do,
To take a crack at

My Ring Dang Doo."

They came by fours, they came by twos,
First came the Japs, then came the Jews,
Then came the sailors, the Marines too,
Till they damn near ruined
Her Ring Dang Doo.

The army came and the army went,
The price went down to fifty cents,
They got the clap and the scabadoo,
When they all took a crack at
Her Ring Dang Doo.

And now she's dead and buried deep,
Her body lies on Chestnut Street,
Her tits hang on the city wall,
And her pussy floats in alcohol.

192. THE RUGBY TINKER

CHORUS: With his bloody great kidney wiper,
And with balls enough for three,
And a yard and a half of foreskin,
Hanging down below his knees.

The lady of the manor was dressing for the ball,
When she spied the rugby tinker tossing off against the wall;

She wrote to him a letter and in it she did say,
"I'd rather be shagged by you, sir, than his lordship
anyday;"

The tinker read the letter and when it he did read,
His balls began to fester and his prick began to bleed;

He mounted on his charger and on it he did ride,
His prick across his saddle and a ball on either side;

He rode into the courtyard and on up to the hall,

"Bloody," cried the valet, "he has come to fuck us all;"

He fucked them in the kitchen and tucked them in the stall,
And the way he shagged the valet was the funniest fuck of all;

The tinker bagged the mistress and in ten minutes she was dead,
With a yard and a half of foreskin firmly wrapped about her head;

He rode from out the manor and on into the street,
With little drops of semen pitter-pattering at his feet;

The tinker he is dead now and buried in St. Paul's,
It took a team of oxen just to drag away his balls;

Some say he went to heaven and some he went to hell,
Some say he shagged the devil and we know he shagged him well.

193. THE S&M MAN

(Sung to the tune of "The Candy Man")

CHORUS: The S&M man,
The S&M man.
The S&M man,
'Cause he does it with love,
Makes the hurt feel good,
  The hurt feel good.

Who can take two icepicks,
(ALL REPEAT)
And stick them in her ears?
(ALL REPEAT)

Rev her up like a Harley and drive her in the rear.

(THIS BEING THE BASIC FORMAT, SING THE FOLLOWING VERSES.)

Who can take a little boy,
And entice him into his car?
Fill 'm full of ludes and let him loose in a gay bar.

Who can take some thumbtacks,
And spread them on the floor?
Make'm dance barefoot 'till their feet are bloody and sore.

Who can take a butcher knife,
And wave it to and fro?
Cut off a little finger and see if it will grow.

Who can take a chicken,
And spread its little legs?
Reach up inside and pull out a dozen eggs.

Who can take a slingshot,
And two coconuts?
Then bend you over and shoot 'em up your butt.

194. THE SEXUAL LIFE OF A CAMEL

CHORUS: Singin' rub titty titty rub titty titty
            titty rub titty rub titty rub
            rub titty rub titty yea.
            Singin' rub titty titty rub titty titty
            titty rub titty rub titty rub
            The assholes are here to stay

            (or)

            We're all queers together,
            Excuse us while we go upstairs, IN PAIRS!.
            We're all queers together,
            And nobody bloody well cares.

The sexual life of the camel is stranger than anyone thinks,
At the height of the mating season he tries to bugger the sphinx.
But the sphinx's posterior sphincter is clogged by the sands of the Nile,
Which accounts for the hump on the camel and the sphinx' inscrutable smile.

The sexual life of the ostrich is stranger than that of man.
At the height of the mating season she buries her head in the sand.
When along comes the male of the species and sees that ass flying high in the air,
He wonder's if it's male or female, and says "What the fuck do I care?!?"

The sexual life of a bullfrog is understood by some,
At the height of the mating season he crawls up the arse of his chum.
But this vile orifice is horrible and filled with foul gases and slime,
Which accounts for his croak and why he says "ugh" all the time.

In the anals of syphulization, from anthropod ape down to man,
It is commonly held that the Navy has buggered whatever it can.
But recent extensive researches, by Darwin and Huxley and Hall,
Conclusively prove that the hedgehog has never been buggered at all.

But theorems were meant to be broken as in the postulate written above,
Regarding the plight of the hedgehog and the boundaries of sexual love.

For a crafty ol' naval bugger left his memoirs to Harvard and Yale,
Simply stating the fact that the hedgehog can be buggered by shaving his tail.

Me daddy drives a motorcar, me mother rides a bike.
Me and me brother we hate each other so I masturbate on his trike.

My name is Bruce you know me, I live in Leicster Square,
With a pair of open toed sandles and a gardenia in me hair.

Me father fucks me mother, me father fucks him back.
And when he's done with her he comes and rams it up me crack.

I went to sell me motorcar, expecting much the worst.
He asked me for my bottom price, I said lets talk about me motorcar first.

This morn' I went to my tailor. He said, "What can I do for you Jack?"
I said, "A pair of velvet trousers with the zipper up the back.!"

I road the puff puff yesterday, There was barely room to stand.
A little boy offered me his seat, so I took it in me hand.

'Twas Christmas eve at harem and the eunuchs all were there,
Observing the vestigial virgins combing their public hair.
When the voice of Father Christmas cam echoing through the hall,
Asking what would you like for Christmas and eunuchs all answered

195 THE STREET OF A THOUSAND ARSE HOLES

CHORUS:
Her greasy twat
Was always hot,
U-Flung-Shit,
Her name, her name,
U-Flung-Shit her name.

In the Street of a Thousand Arse holes
Neath the sign of swinging tit,
There lived a Chinese maiden
By the name of U-Flung-Shit.

She sat beneath the joss sticks
With a smile of celestial bliss,
Her breath like scented lotus,
Her eyes like pools of piss.

She thought of her lover, the bastard,
She thought of her pox ridden beaux,
She thought of the scores she'd had on the floors,
When up walked Won-Hung-Low.

"Oh come to me, you bag of shit."
He cried with tits in hand,
"My love for you will last for hours
Like ice upon the burning sand."

She raised herself on her starboard tit
And gave her tits a tweak,
With smiles in her eyes she stared at him
And said, "Go shit a Peke."

He clutched his tool with calloused hand
And beat it on the walls,
Removed his hat and trampled that
Then danced upon his balls.

At length with anger screaming out
He pissed himself with spleen,
He went and shit and stamped in it
His scrotum turned quite green.

His anger quickly mastered him
He felt with fury black,
She stood on him and bared her quim
And pissed on the bugger's back.

The Chinese maiden now is gone
No longer does she sit,
In the Street of a Thousand Arse Holes
By the sign of the swinging tit.

196. THE TATTOOED LADY

One night in gay Paree
I paid five francs to see
A much tattooed lady
A big fat French lady
Tattooed from head to knee
And on her jaw
Was a British man-o-war
And in the middle of her back
Was a Union Jack
So I paid three francs more
And up and down her spine
Were the old die-hards-in line
And on her big fat bum
Was a picture of the rising sun
And on her fanny
Was Al Jolson singing "Mammy"
How I loves her, how I loves her
My mother-in-law.

I loves my mother-in-law

She is nothing but a dirty old whore
She nags me day and night
I can't do fuck all right
Last night I heard
she was coming round to stay Now isn't it a pity
She only has one titty
And in the family way.
Last night I greased the stairs
Put tin-tacks on the chairs
I hope she breaks her back
Because I do love wearing black
Now Tommy Tucker
Is a stupid little fucker
How I loves her, how I loves her,
How I loves my mother-in-law.

197. THE TINKER

The Lady of the Manor was dressing for the ball,
When she espied a tinker pissing up against the wall.

Chorus :
With his bloody great kidney-wiper,
And his balls the size of three,
And a yard of dirty foreskin, hanging down below his knee.
Hanging down, swinging free, hanging down, we're all thick,
And a yard of dirty foreskin hanging down below his knee.

The lady wrote a letter, and in it she did say,
I'd rather be fucked by a tinker than his Lordship any day.
Chorus

The tinker got the letter, and when it he did read,
His balls began to fester, and his prick began to bleed.
Chorus

He mounted on his charger, and to her place did ride,
With his balls slung o'er his shoulder,
And his prick strapped to his side.

Chorus

He fucked them in the parlour, he fucked them in the hall,
The butler cried, "Gawd save us, he's come to fuck us all."
Chorus

He fucked the groom in the parlour, and the Duchess in her pew,
But then he fucked the butler and the butler's pet mole too.
Chorus

He rode off from the manor, he rode into the street,
Little drops of semen, pitter pattering at his feet.
Chorus

Some say the tinker's gone now, gone fucking down to hell,
All set to fuck the devil, and I bet he fucks him well.
Chorus

198. THE TITANIC

Oh they built a ship Titanic, to sail the ocean blue
and they thought they had a ship that the water'd never go through
But the good Lord raised his hand, said that ship will never land
It was sad when the great ship went down.

Oh they were not far from England, not very far from shore
When the rich refused to associate with the poor
So they put them down below where they'd be the first to go
It was sad when the great ship went down.

The ship was filled with sin and the sides about to burst
When the captain shouted "Women and children first!"
For help they tried to wire but the lines were all on fire
It was sad when the great ship went down.

They threw the life boats out on to the raging sea

As the band struck up with "Nearer my God to Thee."
Little children wept and cried as we threw them over the side
It was sad when the great ship went down.

We were down below trying to make that damn ship go
When the chief shouted out, "Boys she's gonna blow."
We heard a mighty crash and we knew our ass was grassed
It was said when the great ship went down.

The ship began to pitch and the lights began to flicker
and the captain shouted "Me gosh where's me liquor?"
He got completely ripped and went down with the ship
It was sad when the great ship went down.

Lady Astor looked around as she watched her husband drown
And the great Titanic made a gurgling sound
So she wrapped herself in mink as she watched that damn
ship sink
It was sad when the great ship went down.

Duluth and Thunder Bay were scrumming on the deck
When the scrum half shouted "Boys she's gonna wreck!"
So we shouted out with fear, "GIMME ANOTHER BEER!"
It was sad when the great ship went down.

So they built another ship Titanic Number Two
And they thought they had a ship that the water'd never go
through
But they christened it with beer and it sank right off the pier
It was sad when the great ship went down.

The moral of the story is very plain to see
Always wear your life preserver when you go out to sea
The Titanic never made it and never more shall be
It was sad when the great ship went down.

Intermix these....

Husbands and wives

little children lost their lives
Uncles and aunts
little children lost their pants
Sisters and brothers
everybody fucked each other
Brothers and sisters
Fucked until they all had blisters

199. THE TULAGI SONG

CHORUS: Fuck'em all, fuck'em all,
                  The long and the short and the tall,
                  There'll be no promotions this side of the
ocean,
                  The tucking reserves got 'em all.

So we asked the Army to come to Tulagi,
General MacArthur said no,
He gave us the reason, it wasn't the season,
Besides there's no USO.

So we asked the Air Force to come to Tulagi,
The Air Force was quick to agree,
They bombed out my bunkie, two dogs and one donkey,
And seven platoons of jireens.

So we asked the Coast Guard to come to Tulagi,
The Coast Guard didn't appear,
They sent us a letter, said we like it here better,
Maybe we'll make it next year.

So we asked the Navy to come to Tulagi,
The Navy was pleased and agreed,
From four directions, with forty sections,
Oh what a fucked up stampede.

So we asked the Nurses to come to Tulagi,

The Nurses were quick to appease,
Their asses on tables, all bearing the labels,
Reserved for the officers please.

So here's to your corporals and all your 01's,
Here's to your sergeants and their bastard sons,
As we fondly do bid them farewell,
The long and the short and the tall,
There'll be no promotions this side of the ocean,
The tucking reserves got 'em all.

200. THE TWELVE DAYS OF CHRISTMAS

On the first day of Christmas, my true love gave to me,
A blow job in a pear tree

On the second day of ....
Two sweaty gonads
Three French letters
Four inches wet
Five dripping cunts
Six shooting hard ons
Seven shrivelled testes
Eight maidens bleeding
Nine knobs a-throbbing
Ten twats a-twitching
Eleven empty scrotums
Twelve fairies fucking

201. THE VIRGIN STURGEON

CHORUS: My ruddy oath it is,
                My ruddy oath it is.

Caviar comes from the virgin sturgeon,

The virgin sturgeon is a very fine fish,
The virgin sturgeon needs no urgin',
That's why caviar is my dish.

I gave caviar to my girlfriend,
She was a virgin tried and true,
Ever since she had the caviar,
There ain't nothing she won't do.

I gave caviar to my grandpa,
Grandpa's age is ninety-three,
And next time I saw grandpa,
He'd chased grandma up a tree.

I gave caviar to my bow-wow,
All the others looked agog,
He had what those bitches wanted,
Wasn't he a lucky dog?

My father was a lighthouse keeper,
He had caviar for his tea,
He had three children by a mermaid,
Two were Rippers, one was me.

Oysters are prolific bivalves,
Rear their young ones in their shell,
How they priddle is a riddle,
But they do, so what the hell.

The female clam is optimistic,
Shoots her eggs out in the sea,
She hopes her suitor as a shooter,
Hits the self-same spot as she.

202. THE WALRUS AND THE CARPENTER

If all the whores with dirty drawers
Were lying in the Strand
Do you suppose, the Walrus said
That we could raise a stand?
I doubt it, said the Carpenter
But wouldn't it be grand
And all the while the dirty sod
Was coming in his hand.

When you were only sweet sixteen
And had a little quim
You stood before the looking-glass
And put one finger in
But now that you are old and grey
And losing all your charm
I can get five fingers in
And half my fucking arm.

203. THE WILD ROVER

(Sung to the tune of "Wild Rover")

CHORUS: And it's no nay never, no nay never no
more

          Will I play the wild rover, no never no more.

I've been a wild rover for many a year
And I spent all my money on whisky and beer
But now I'm returning with gold in great store
And I swear I will play the wild rover no more.

I went to an ale-house I used to frequent
And I told the landlady my money was spent
I asked her for credit she answered me no
It's custom like yours I can get any day.

I took from my pocket sovereigns so bright
That the landlady's eyes opened wide with delight
She said she had whisky and beer of the best
And the words that she spoke were only in jest.

I'll go to my parents, confess what I've done
And ask them to pardon their prodigal son
And when they forgive me as ofttimes as before
Then I swear I will play the wild rover no more.

204. THE WILD WEST SHOW

CHORUS: We're off to see the Wild West Show,
               The elephants and the kangaroos,
               No matter what the weather as long as
we're together,
               We're off to see the Wild West Show.

...   Ladies and gentlemen,
           In this corner we have the Oh No Bird.
           The Oh No Bird has legs three inches long,
           But has testicles which hang down six inches,
           And whenever it comes in for a landing,
           It goes, "Oh no, oh no, oh no."

...   Ladies and gentlemen,
           In this corner we have the Crash Bam Bam Bam
Bird.
           The Crash Bam Bam Bam Bird is a very close
relative
           to the aforementioned Oh No Bird,
           But unlike the Oh No Bird,
           The Crash Bam Bam Bam Bird only roosts on
corrugated tin roofs,
           And when it comes in for a landing it goes crash
bam bam bam.

...   Ladies and gentlemen,

In this corner we have Lulu the tattooed lady.
She has a "W" tattooed on one side of her ass,
And she has a "W" tattooed on the other side of her ass,
A.nd when she stands up it spells "WOW,"
And when she stands on her hands it spells "MOM,"
And when she does cartwheels it spells "WOW, MOM, WOW."

... Ladies and gentlemen,
In this corner we have Lulu the tattooed lady's sister.
On the inside of one thigh she has "MERRY CHRISTMAS" tattooed,
And on the inside of the other thigh she has "HAPPY NEW YEAR" tattooed,
And she invites all of you to come between the holidays.

... Ladies and gentlemen,
In this corner we have the Fuckgowee Tribe.
The Fuckgowee Tribe lives in deepest, darkest Africa,
In a land of six feet tall grass,
But the Fuckgowee Tribe stand only three feet tall,
And they go around all day saying "Where the fuck are we, where the fuck are we'?"

... Ladies and gentlemen,
In this corner we have the Mathematical Impossibility.
Yes, ladies and gentlemen,
The Mathematical Impossibility is the only girl in the whole world,
Who was ate before she was seven.

... Ladies and gentlemen,
In this corner we have the Admiral's Daughter.
Yes, the infamous Admiral's Daughter.

She is the final resting place for discharged semen.

...   Ladies and gentlemen,
In this comer we have the Ch-Ch-Christ Bird.
This bird has one wing half as long as the other,
Thus it flies in ever decreasing concentric circles,
Until it flies up its own anal orifice, .
And then shouts, "Ch-Ch-Christ it's dark in here."

...   Ladies and gentlemen,
In this corner we have the Bengal Tiger.
The Bengal Tiger is the only pussy in the whole world that eats you.

...   Ladies and gentlemen,
In this corner we have the Dentist.
The Dentist is the only man you have to pay to put his tools in your mouth.

205. THE WOMAN MARINE HYMN

(Sung to the tune of "Davey Crockett")

CHORUS: Rosey, Rosey Rottencrotch,
                    Pride of the Women Marines.

Born in a whorehouse, in Oceanside,
So ticking ugly, her mother cried.
Lived in a shack, on old North Hill,
Before the age of five, they had her on the pill.

At age seventeen, she joined the Corps,
Became like the rest, a duty whore.
Thought she was better, a superior lass,
I jumped up and told her, kiss my ass.

We sent her to school, they didn't teach her shit,
When she got out, she thought she was it.
Became the Gunner's favorite, his number one runt,
But we all know, she's just a slimy cunt.

Because her cheeks, were a little pink,
She was convinced, her shit didn't stink.
They made her a corporal, an NCO,
But all she did right, was give a good blow.

206. THERE WAS A LASS OF ISLINGTON

There was a Lass of *Islington*,
As I have heard many tell;
And she would to Fair *London* go,
Fine Apples and Pears to sell:
And as along the Streets she flung,
With her basket on her Arm:
Her Pears to sell, you may know it right well,
This fair Maid meant no harm.
But as she tript along the Street,
Her pleasant Fruit to sell;
A Vintner did with her meet,
Who lik'd this Maid full well:
Quoth he, fair Maid, what have you there?
In Basket decked brave;
Fine Pears, quoth she, and if it please ye
A taste Sir you shall have.
The Vintner he took a Taste,
And lik'd it well, for why;
This Maid he thought of all the rest,
Most pleasing to his Eye:
Quoth he, fair Maid I have a Suit,
That you to me must grant;
Which if I find you be so kind,
Nothing that you shall want.
Thy Beauty doth so please my Eye,
And dazles so my sight;
That now of all my Liberty,
I am deprived quite:

Then prithee now consent to me,
And do not put me by;
It is but one small courtesie,
All Night with you to lie.
Sir, if you lie with me one Night,
As you propound to me;
I do expect that you should prove,
Both courteous, kind and free:
And for to tell you all in short,
It will cost you Five Pound,
A Match, a Match, the Vintner said,
And so let this go round.
When he had lain with her all Night,
Her Money she did crave,
O stay, quoth he, the other Night,
And thy Money thou shalt have:
I cannot stay, nor I will not stay,
I needs must now be gone,
Why then thou may'st thy Money go look,
For Money I'll pay thee none.
This Maid she made no more ado,
But to a Justice went;
And unto him she made her moan,
Who did her Case lament:
She said she had a Cellar Let out,
To a Vintner in the Town;
And how that he did then agree
Five Pound to pay her down.
But now, quoth she, the Case is thus,
No Rent that he will pay;
Therefore your Worship I beseech,
To send for him this Day:
Then strait the Justice for him sent,
And asked the Reason why;
That he would pay this Maid no Rent?
To which he did Reply,

Although I hired a Cellar of her,
And the Possession was mine?
I ne'er put any thing into it,
But one poor Pipe of Wine:
Therefore my Bargain it was hard,
As you may plainly see;
I from my Freedom was Debarr'd,
Then good Sir favour me.
This Fair Maid being ripe of Wit,
She strait Reply'd again;
There were two Butts more at the Door,
Why did you not roul them in?
You had your Freedom and your Will,
As is to you well known;
Therefore I do desire still,
For to receive my own.
The Justice hearing of their Case,
Did then give Order strait;
That he the Money should pay down,
She should no longer wait:
Withal he told the Vintner plain
If he a Tennant be;
He must expect to pay the same,
For he could not sit Rent-free.
But when the Money she had got,
She put it in her Purse:
And clapt her Hand on the Cellar Door,
And said it was never the worse:
Which caused the People all to laugh,
To see this Vintner Fine:
Out-witted by a Country Girl,
About his Pipe of Wine.

balls.

207. THERE WAS A PRIEST, THE DIRTY BEAST

There was a priest, the dirty beast,
Whose name was Alexander.
His mighty prick was inches thick
He called it Salamander.

One night he slept with the Gypsy Queen,
Whose face was black as charcoal,
But in the dark he missed his mark,
And sparks came out her arse hole.

A brat was born one rainy morn,
With a face as black as charcoal,
It had a prick ten inches thick
But it didn't have an arse hole.

208. THERE WAS A YOUNG SAILOR

There was a young sailor who sat on a rock
Wailing his fists and abusing his...
Navel, a neighboring tavern was watching his fits
Teaching his children to play with their..-
Kites and their marbles as in days of yore
Along came a woman who looked like a...
Decent young lady who walked like a duck
She said she was learning a new way to...
Bring up the children and teach them to knit
While the boys in the barnyard were shoveling...
The contents of pigsty muck and the mire
The squire of the manor was pulling his...
Horse from the stable to go to the hunt
His wife in the boudoir was powdering her...
Nose and arranging her vanity box
And taking precautions to ward off the...
Gout and rhuematics which makes her feel stiff

Too well did she remember her last dose of..
What did you think I was going to say?
No you rude bugger that's all for today.

209. THERE WAS AN OLD WOMAN LIV'D UNDER A HILL

There was an old Woman liv'd under a Hill,
Sing Trolly lolly, lolly, lolly, lo;
She had good Beer and Ale for to sell,
Ho, ho, had she so, had she so, had she so;
She had a Daughter her name was *Siss*,
Sing Trolly lolly, lolly, lolly, lo;
She kept her at Home for to welcome her Guest,
Ho, ho, did she so, did she so, did she so.
There came a Trooper riding by,
Sing trolly, *&c.*
He call'd for Drink most plentifully,
Ho, ho, did he so, *&c.*
When one Pot was out he call'd for another,
Sing trolly, *&c.*
He kiss'd the Daughter before the Mother,
Ho, ho, did he so, *&c.*
And when Night came on to Bed they went,
Sing trolly, *&c.*
It was with the Mother's own Consent,
Ho, ho, was it so, *&c.*
Quoth she what is this so stiff and warm,
Sing trolly *&c.*
'Tis Ball my Nag he will do you no harm,
Ho, ho, wont he so, *&c.*
But what is this hangs under his Chin,
Sing trolly, *&c.*
'Tis the Bag he puts his Provender in,
Ho, ho, is it so, *&c.*
Quoth he what is this? Quoth she 'tis a Well,

Sing trolly, *&c.*
Where Ball your Nag may drink his fill,
Ho, ho, may he so, *&c.*
But what if my Nag should chance to slip in,
Sing trolly, *&c.*
Then catch hold of the Grass that grows on the brim,
Ho, ho, must I so, *&c.*
But what if the Grass should chance to fail,
Sing trolly, *&c.*
Shove him in by the Head, pull him out by the Tail,
Ho, ho, must I so, *&c.*

210. THESE FOOLISH THINGS

(Tune of my favorite things)

Ten pounds of titty in a loose brassiere
Your twat a-twitchin like a moose's ear
Ejaculations in my glass of beer
These foolish things remind me of you, Dear.

Naked color photographs of Liberace
The way you say to me "Come lick my crotchy"
Syphilitic scabs that make my face all blotchy
These foolish things remind me of you, Dear.

A pubic hair in my breakfast roll
A bloody Kotex in my toilet bowl
The festic odor of your pink asshole
These foolish things remind me of you, Dear.

An unborn fetus on a marble slab
Erected penis with a broken scab
A sloppy blow job in a taxi cab
These foolish things remind me of you, Dear.

211. THEY'RE DIGGING UP DAD'S REMAINS

They're digging up dad's remains to build a sewer;
They're doing the job regardless of expense;
They're digging up dad's remains to make way for ten inch drains
To satisfy some rich man's residence, 'gor blieme!

Now father in his lifetime wasn't a quitter, a quitter;
And I don't suppose he'll be a quitter now;
Cause he'll dress up in a sheet and he'll haunt the shithouse seat
And only let them toffs go when he allows, 'gor blieme!

Now won't there be some horrible constipation;
Oh won't the loose bound toffs oh rack and rave;
But it serves them bloody well right
For having the perishing nerve to muck about with a British workman's grave.

212. THOSE OLD RED FLANNEL DRAWERS THAT MAGGIE WORE

CHORUS: Those old red flannel drawers that Maggie wore.

They were tattered, they were torn,
Round the crotch piece they were worn.

They were rotten down the front,
With the dripping of her cunt.

She put them in the sink,
My God, there was a stink.

They were hemmed in, they were tucked in,
They were the drawers that she was married in.

She put them on the mat,
And paralysed the cat.

She hung them on the line,
And the sun refused to shine.

She buried them in the ground,
Killed the grass for miles around.

213. THRASHING MACHINE

'Twas way down in Devon that I did hear tell,
I first set my eyes on our little Nell,
She was so pretty and only sixteen,
When I ups and I shows 'er my Thrashing Machine.

Chorus ;
I 'ad 'er, I 'ad 'er, I 'ad 'er I ay,
I 'ad 'er, I 'ad 'er, I 'ad 'er I ay,
I 'ad 'er by night and I 'ad 'er by day,
And I ups and I shows 'er the West Country way.

The barn door was open and I steps inside,
Some hay in the corner I espied,
She worked the throttle and I worked the steam,
When I ups and I shows 'er my Thrashing Machine.
Chorus

Oh father, oh father, I've come to confess,
I've left a young maid in a hell of a mess,
Her blouse is all tattered, her tits are all bare,
And there's something inside her that shouldn't be there.
Chorus

Oh son, oh son, you should have known better,
To woo a fair maid without a french letter,
Oh father, oh father, you do me unjust,
I used one of yours and the fucking thing bust.

Chorus

Six months later all is not well,
The poor little maid is beginning to swell,
And under her apron can clearly be seen,
The terrible works of my Thrashing Machine.
 Chorus

Nine months later all has gone well,
A new little babe for our little Nell,
And under his nappy can clearly be seen,
A brand new two cylinder Thrashing Machine.
 Chorus

214. THREE GERMAN OFFICERS

(Sung to the tune of "Inky, Dinky, Parlez-veus")

Three German officers crossed the Rhine,
Parlez-veus,
Three German officers crossed the Rhine,
Parlez-veus,
Three German officers crossed the Rhine,
They fucked the women and drank the wine,
Inky, dinky, parlez-veus.

They came upon a wayside inn,
Shit on the mat and walked right in.

Oh landlord have you a daughter fair,
Lily-white tits and golden hair?

At last they got her on a bed,
Fucked her till her cheeks were red.

And then they took her to a shed,
Fucked her till she was nearly dead.

They took her down a shady lane,
Fucked her back to life again.

They took her up in an aeroplane,
Squeezed her tits and made it rain.

They fucked her up, they fucked her down,
They tucked her right around the town.

They fucked her in, they fucked her out,
They fucked her up her waterspout.

Now she lives in our town,
Sells her cunt for half a crown.

Seven months went and all was well,
Eight months went and she started to swell.

Nine months went and she gave a grunt,
And a little white bugger popped out her cunt.

The little white bugger he grew and grew,
He fucked his mother and sister too.

The little white bugger he went to hell,
He fucked the Devil and his wife as well.

215. THREE JEWS FROM JERUSALEM

There were three Jews from Jerusalem,
There were three Jews from Jerusalem
JERRY-JERRY-JERRY-USALEM,
JERRY-JERRY-JERRY-USALEM
There were three Jews from Jerusalem.

The first one's name was Issac, the first one's name was
Issac,
EYSIE-EYSIE-EYSIE-SUCK-SUCK-SUCK, EYSIE-EYSIE-
EYSIE-SUCK-SUCK-SUCK
The first one's name was Issac.

The second one's name was Joseph,
The second one's name was Joseph,
JOSIE-JOSIE-JOSIE-SIPH-SIPH-SIPH, JOSIE-JOSIE-JOSIE-SIPH-SIPH-SIPH
The second one's name was Joseph.

The third one's name was Jehosaphat,
The third one's name was Jehosaphat,
JOSIE-JOSIE-JOSIE-FART-FART-FART,
JOSIE-JOSIE-JOSIE-FART-FART-FART
The third one's name was Jehosaphat.

They went for a ride in a charabang,
They went for a ride in a charabang,
CHARA-CHARA-CHARA-BANG-BANG-BANG, CHARA-CHARA-CHARA-BANG-BANG-BANG
They went for a ride in a Charabang.

There was a mighty thunderclap,
There was a mighty thunderclap,
THUNDER-THUNDER-THUNDER-CLAP-CLAP-CLAP,
THUNDER-THUNDER-THUNDER-CLAP-CLAP-CLAP
There was a mighty thunderclap.

The car went over a precipice, the car went over a precipice,
PRECI-PRECI-PRECI-PISS-PISS-PISS, PRECI-PRECI-PRECI-PISS-PISS-PISS
The car went over a Precipice.

They were taken off to hospital,
They were taken off to hospital,
HOSI-HOSI-HOSI-TOOL-TOOL-TOOL, HOSI-HOSI-HOSI-TOOL-TOOL-TOOL
They were taken off to hospital.

The hospital was in Norfolk, the hospital was in Norfolk,
NORI-NORI-NORI-FUCK-FUCK-FUCK,
NORI-NORI-NORI-FUCK-FUCK-Fuck
The hospital was in Norfolk.

There were no beds a-vacant, there were no beds a-vacant,
VAY-AY-AY-AY-CUNT-CUNT-CUNT,
VAY-AY-AY-AY-CUNT-CUNT-Cunt
There were no beds vacant.

They laid them on a palliasse, they laid them on a palliasse,
PALLY-ALLY-ALLY-ARSE-ARSE-ARSE, PALLY-ALLY-ALLY-
ARSE-ARSE-ARSE,
They laid them on a palliasse.

This is where we finish it, this is where we finish it,
FINI-FINI-FINI-SHIT-SHIT-SHIT,
FINI-FINI-FINI-SHIT-SHIT-SHIT
This is where we finish it.

216. THREE OLD WHORES FROM WINNIPEG

CHORUS: Oh, rolly poly stick-a my holey,
Up my slimy slough,
I drag my balls across the halls,
I'm one of the sportin' crew.

Tree old whores from Winnipeg
Were drinking cherry wine,
Says one of them to the other two,
"Yours is smaller than mine."

"You're a liar," says the second old whore,
"Mine's as big as the sea,
Ships sail in and ships sail out
And never bother me."

"You're a liar," says the third old whore,
"Mine's as big as the moon
Ships sail in on the first of the year
And never come out till June."

"You're a liar," say the first again,
Mine's as big as the air,
Ships sail in and ships sail out
And never tickle a hair."

"You're a liar," says the second again,
"Mine is bigger than all,
For many's the ship that sails right in
And never comes out at all."

217. TROJAN IS A GIRL'S BEST FRIEND

A poke with a bloke may be quite incidental,
Trojan is a girl's best friend,
You may get the works
But you won't be parental.
As he slides it in,
You trust that good old latex skin,
As he lets fly, none gets by
'Cos it's all gathered up in the end.
This little precaution
Avoids an abortion.
Trojan is a girl's best friend.

218. UNHAPPY BELLA

Bella was young and Bella was fair,
With bright blue eyes and golden hair,
O unhappy Bella!
Her step was light and her heart was gay,
But she had no sense, and one fine day
She got herself put in the family way
By a wicked, heartless, cruel deceiver.

Poor Bella was young, she didn't believe

That the world is hard and men deceive,
O unhappy Bella!
She said, "My man will do what's just,
He'll marry me now, because he must."
Her heart was full of loving trust
In a wicked, heartless, cruel deceiver.

She went to his house; the dirty skunk
Had packed his bags and done a bunk,
O unhappy Bella!
Her landlady said, "Get out, you whore,
I won't have your sort a-darkening my door."
Poor Bella was put to affliction sore
By a wicked, heartless, cruel deceiver.

All night she tramped the cruel snows,
What she must have suffered nobody knows,
O unhappy Bella!
And when the morning dawned so red,
Alas, alas, poor Bella was dead,
Sent so young to her lonely bed
By a wicked, heartless, cruel deceiver.

So thus, you see, do what you will,
The fruits of sin are suffering still,
O unhappy Bella!
As into the grave they laid her low,
The men said, "Alas, but life is so."
But the women chanted, sweet and low,
"It's all the men, the dirty bastards!"

219. US DEVON BOYS

Us Devon boys have hairy ears,
We piss through leather breeches,
We wipe our arse on broken glass, us hardy sons of bitches.

When cunt is rare we fuck a bear, we knife him if he
snitches,

We knock our cocks against the rocks,
Us hardy sons of bitches.

We wipe our arse upon the grass, in bushes or in ditches,
Our two pound cocks are full of knots,
Us hardy sons of bitches.

Without remorse we fuck a horse, and beat him if he twitches,
Our two foot dicks are full of nicks, us hardy sons of bitches.

To make a mule stand for the tool,
We beat him with hickory switches,
We use our pricks for walking sticks, us hardy sons of bitches.

Great joy we reap from fucking sheep,
In barns or bogs or ditches,
Nor give a damn if it be a ram, us hardy sons of bitches.

We walk around, prick to the ground, and kick it if it itches,
And if it throbs, we scratch with cobs, us hardy sons of bitches.

220. VICTORY SONG

We don't play for adoration,
We don't play for vIctory.
We just play for inspiration,
We're the_____ R.F.C.
Balls to _____.
Balls to _____.
We won't play you anymore.
We won't play you anymore.

221. VIRGIN STURGEON

Caviar comes from the virgin sturgeon,
The virgin sturgeon's a very fine fish,
The virgin sturgeon needs no 'urgin,
That's why caviar is my dish.

I gave caviar to my girl friend,
she was a virgin tried and true,
Ever since she had that caviar,
There 'aint nothing she won't do,

I gave caviar to my grandpa,
Grandpa's age is ninety three,
The very next time I saw my grandpa,
He'd chased grandma up a tree.

My father was a lighthouse keeper,
He had caviar for his tea,
He had three children by a mermaid,
Two were kippers, one was me.

I gave caviar to my bow-wow, all the others looked agog,
He had what those bitches wanted,
Wasn't he a lucky dog.

The female clam is optimistic, shoots her eggs out in the
sea,
She hopes her suitor as a shooter,
Hits the selfsame spot as she.

Oysters are prolific bi-valves,
Rear their young ones in their shell,
How they piddle is a riddle, but they do so what the hell.

222. WAYWARD BOY

I walked the street with my prick to my feet,
I heard a voice come to me,

A lovely maid looked out and said,
"I need someone to screw me !"
Said I, "My dear, you needn't fear,
For I have heard your pleading,
It's very plain I can ease your pain,
I've got just what you're needing."

I've heard of you, my wayward boy,
Your name is known quite widely,
But I can't come down, I'm sad to say,
My door is bolted tightly.
My father is a Minister, my maidenhead does cherish,
So every night he locks me tight, so horny do I perish.

She stood out there in the midnight air,
With the wind blowing up her hinder,
And her arse all bare and her cunt all hair,
So I climbed up right behind her.
Said I, "Young maid, don't be afraid,
The pleasures can be thrilling,
If you're someone who wants some fun,
The wayward boy is willing."

She jumped into bed and covered up her head,
And she swore that I couldn't find her,
But I knew damned well she lied like hell,
So I jumped in right behind her.
I shoved old Pete right through the sheet,
And up her organ grinder, the white of an egg ran down her
leg,
And the rest remained inside her.

On the very next stroke, the damn bed broke,
Her father came a-gunning,
I hit the floor with my prick all sore,
I got to my feet a-running.
I left that lass in my bare arse, as a shotgun blast did find
me,
For weeks in bed I was picking out lead,

With a mirror held behind me.

As years went by, I thought with a sigh,
When fancy did remind me,
So one fine day I made my way, to the girl I left behind me,
She was still locked in to keep off men,
She didn't look much older,
But she'd had her joys; three girls, four boys,
And a baby on her shoulder.

223. WE ARE WARRIORS

CHORUS: We are warriors!
                   Mighty, mighty warriors,
                   We have bullets,
                   And we got rifles.

We went hunting,
Came upon a river,
Couldn't go under it,
Couldn't go over it,
Couldn't go around it,
Had to go through it!

We went hunting,
Came upon a mountain,
Couldn't go under it,
Couldn't go over it,
Couldn't go around it,
Had to go through it!

We went hunting,
Came upon a woman!
Couldn't go under her,
Couldn't go over her,
Couldn't go around her,
HAD TO GO THROUGH HER!

224. WE WISH YOU A SHAG AT CHRISTMAS

We wish you a shag at Christmas,
We wish you a shag at Christmas,
We wish you a shag at Christmas, and all through the year.

Chorus:
Rubber johnies we bring to stuff up her quim,
We wish you a hump at Christmas and all through the year.

Now bring us some lusty women
Now bring us some lusty women
Now bring us some lusty women, and bring them out here.
Chorus

For we all like a bit of poking,
For we all like a bit of poking,
For we all like a bit of poking, so bring them out here.
Chorus

We won't go until we shag 'em,
We won't go until we shag 'em,
We won't go until we shag 'em, so bring them out here.
Chorus

I likes it when she sucks it,
I likes it when she sucks it,
I likes it when she sucks it, so why not suck here.
Chorus

225. WEE WEE SONG

When I was just a wee wee tot,
They took me from my wee wee cot,
Put me on my wee wee pot, to see if I could wee or not.
When they found that I could not,

They took me from my wee wee pot,
Put me in my wee wee cot, where I wee weed quite a lot.
Now I'm old and getting grey, I can only wee wee once a day.

226. WHAT SHALL WE DO WITH A HOMO SAILOR ?

Chorus :
Hooray and up she rises, hooray and up she rises,
Hooray and up she rises, early in the morning.
What shall we do with a homo sailor,
What shall we do with a homo sailor,
What shall we do with a homo sailor, early in the morning.

Put him in bed with the captain's daughter,
Put him in bed with the captain's daughter,
Put him in bed with the captain's daughter,
Early in the morning.
Chorus

Tie him by his bollocks to the mainsail,
Tie him by his bollocks to the mainsail,
Tie him by his bollocks to the mainsail, early in the morning.
Chorus
Encourage him to shag a dead donkey,
Encourage him to shag a dead donkey,
Encourage him to shag a dead donkey, early in the morning.
Chorus

Walk the plank being buggered by his bum-boy,
Walk the plank being buggered by his bum-boy,
Walk the plank being buggered by his bum-boy,
Early in the morning.
Chorus

Shave his pubes with a rusty razor,
Shave his pubes with a rusty razor,
Shave his pubes with a rusty razor, early in the morning.
Chorus

Bugger him with the ship's main cannon,
Bugger him with the ship's main cannon,
Bugger him with the ship's main cannon,
Early in the morning.
Chorus

227. WHEN FOR AIR I TAKE MY MARE

When for Air
I take my Mare,
And mount her first,
She walks just thus,
Her Head held low,
And Motion slow;
With Nodding, Plodding,
Wagging, Jogging,
Dashing, Plashing,
Snorting, Starting,
Whimsically she goes:
Then Whip stirs up,
Trot, Trot, Trot;
Ambling then with easy slight,
She riggles like a Bride at Night;
Her shuffling hitch,
Regales my Britch;
Whilst Trott, Trott, Trott, Trott,
Brings on the Gallop,
The Gallop, the Gallop,
The Gallop, and then a short
Trott, Trott, Trott, Trott,
Straight again up and down,
Up and down, up and down,
Till she comes home with a Trott,
When Night dark grows.

Just so *Phillis*,
Fair as Lillies,
As her Face is,
Has her Paces;
And in Bed too,
Like my Pad too;
Nodding, Plodding,
Wagging, Jogging,
Dashing, Plashing,
Flirting, Spirting,
Artful are all her ways:
Heart thumps pitt, patt,
Trott, Trott, Trott, Trott:
Ambling, then her Tongue gets loose,
Whilst wrigling near I press more close:
Ye Devil she crys,
I'll tear your Eyes,
When Main seiz'd,
Bum squeez'd,
I Gallop, I Gallop, I Gallop, I Gallop,
And Trott, Trott, Trott, Trott,
Streight again up and down,
Up and down, up and down,
Till the last Jerk with a Trot,
Ends our Love Chase.

228. WHEN LADY JANE BECAME A TART

It fairly broke the family's heart
When Lady Jane became a tart
But blood is blood and race is race
And so to save the family face
They bought her an expensive flat
With "Welcome" written on the mat.

It was not long ere Lady Jane

Brought her patrician charms to fame
A clientele of sahibs pukka
Who regularly came to fuck her,
And it was whispered without malice
She had a client from the palace.

No one could nestle in her charms
Unless he wore ancestral arms
No one to her could gain an entry,
Unless he were of the landed gentry,
And so before her sun had set
She'd worked her way through Debrett.

When Lady Anne became a whore
It grieved the family even more,
But they felt they couldn't do the same
As they had done for Lady Jane,
So they bought her an exclusive beat,
On the shady side of Jermyn Street.

When Lord St. Clancy Became a nancy
It did not please the family fancy
And so in order to protect him
They did inscribe upon his rectum,
"All commoners must now drive steerage,
This arse hole is reserved for peerage."

229. WHOREDEAN

We are from Whoredean, good girls are we,
We take a pride in our virginity,
We take precautions, Like having abortions,
For we are from Whoredean school.

Chorus ; Up school, Up school, Up school,
Right Up School, SHIT !
La dee da, two fingers up your crutch,
La dee da, three fingers are too much. Hey !

When we go to the beach for a swim,
People remark on the size of our quim,
You can bet your bottom dollar,
It's like a horse's collar, for we are from Whoredean school.
Chorus

Our Headmaster, he is a fool,
He's really got a gi-normous tool,
It's alright for tunnels, and Queen Mary's funnels,
But no good for Whoredean school.
 Chorus

Our math's master, he is a fool,
He's only got a teeny weeny tool,
It's alright for keyholes, and little girlies wee holes,
But no good for Whoredean school.
 Chorus

Our gym mistress, she is the best,
She teaches us to develop our chest,
We wear tight sweaters, and carry french letters,
For we are from Whoredean school.
 Chorus

Our French mistress, her name is Jane,
She only likes it now and again,
And again and again, and again and again,
For we are from Whoredean school.
 Chorus

At the bottom of our garden there lives a tramp,
He is a deserter from the local army camp,
We call him Hector, vagina inspector,
For we are from Whoredean school.
 Chorus

Our Headmistress, you cannot beat,
She lets us go out walking the street,
We sell our titties, for threepenny bitties,

For we are from Whoredean school.
 Chorus

You may sleep upon the floor (3 times)
Cried the fair young maiden.
Oh bugger the floor you dirty old whore,
Cried Barnacle Bill the Sailor. (twice)

You may sleep upon the mat (3 times)
Cried the fair young maiden.
Oh bugger the mat you can't fuck that,
Cried Barnacle Bill the Sailor. (twice)

You may sleep upon the stairs (3 times)
Cried the fair young maiden.
Oh bugger the stairs they haven't got hairs,
Cried Barnacle Bill the Sailor. (twice)

230. WHY WAS HE BORN SO BEAUTIFUL?

Why was he born so beautiful?
Why was he born at all?
He's no fucking use to anyone,
He's no ducking use at all. (or: He's only got one ball.)

So drink Mother-Fucker, Drink Mother-Fucker, Drink Mother-Fucker Drink!
So drink Mother-Fucker, Drink Mother-Fucker, Drink Mother-Fucker Drink!

231. WILL YOU MARRY ME?

(FIRST VERSE IS SUNG IN MASCULINE VOICE AND REPLY VERSE IS SUNG IN
A FEMININE VOICE.)

If I give you half-a-crown, can I take your knickers down?
Will you marry marry marry marry, will you marry me?

If you give me half-a-crown, you can't take my knickers down.
You can't marry marry marry marry, you can't marry me.

If I give you fish and chips, will you let me squeeze your tits?
Will you marry marry marry marry, will you marry me?

If you give me fish and chips, I won't let you squeeze my tits.
You can't marry marry marry marry, you can't marry me.

If I gargle with Lavoris, can I suck on your clitoris?
Will you marry marry marry marry, will you marry me?

If you gargle with Lavoris, you can't suck on my clitoris.
You can't marry marry marry marry, you can't marry me.

If I give you half-a-note, can I shove it down your throat?
Will you marry marry marry marry, will you marry me?

If you give me half-a-note, you can't shove it down my throat.
You can't marry marry marry marry, you can't marry me.

If I give you a pound of grass, can I shove it up your ass?
Will you marry marry marry marry, will you marry me?

If you give me a pound of grass, you can't shove it up my ass.
You can't marry marry marry marry, you can't marry me.

If I give you half-a-quid, will you suck on my big squid?
Will you marry marry marry marry, will you marry me?

If you give me half-a-quid, I won't suck on your big squid.
You can't marry marry marry marry, you can't marry me.

If I give you a whole crown, will you blow me till you drown?

Will you marry marry marry marry, will you marry me?

If you give me a whole crown, I won't blow you till I drown.
You can't marry marry marry marry, you can't marry me.

If I give you silk and lace, can I spray it in your face?
Will you marry marry marry marry, will you marry me?

If you give me silk and lace, you can't spray it in my face.
You can't marry marry marry marry, you can't marry me.

if I give you my big chest, and all the money that I possess,
Will You marry marry marry marry, will you marry me?

If you give me your big chest, and all the money that you possess,
I will marry marry marry marry, I will marry you.

Get out the door, you lousy whore, my money was all you were looking for.
I'll not marry marry marry marry, I'll not marry you.

232. WOODPECKER SONG

I put my finger in the woodpecker's hole
And the woodpecker cried, "God bless my soul,
Take it out, take it out, take it out,
Remove it."

I removed my finger from the woodpecker's hole
And the woodpecker cried, "God bless my soul,
Put it back, put it back, put it back,
Replace it."

I replaced my finger in the woodpecker's hole
And the woodpecker cried, "God bless my soul,
Turn it round, turn it round, turn it round,
Revolve it."

I revolved my finger in the woodpecker's hole
And the woodpecker cried, "God bless my soul,
Turn it bout, turn it bout, turn it bout
Reverse it."

I reversed my finger in the woodpecker's hole
And the woodpecker cried, "God bless my soul,
In and out, in and out, in and out,
Rotate it."

I rotated my finger in the woodpecker's hole
And the woodpecker said, "God bless my soul,
Pull it out, pull it out, pull it out,
Retract it."

I retracted my finger from the woodpecker's hole
And the woodpecker said, "God bless my soul,
Take a whiff, take a whiff, take a whiff."
REVOLTING!

233. WORKING DOWN THE SEWER

CHORUS: Workin' down the sewer
           shovellin' up manure,
           That's the way the soldier
           does his bit, shovelling shit.
           You can hear the shovels ring
           with a ting-a-ling-a-ling,
           When you're working down
           the sewer with the gang.

Now the foreman said to me,
As he grabbed me by the arse,
"You're the dirtiest little bastard
That we have upon the job.
Your wages for the week
Will be five and twenty bob,
When you're working down

the sewer with the gang."

One morning after eight,
When I turned up at the gate,
The foreman said to me,
"Now fucking look 'ere mate,
If you won't come fucking early
Then you can't come fucking late,
When you're workin' down
the sewer with the gang."

234. WOULD YE HAVE A YOUNG VIRGIN OF FIFTEEN YEARS

Would ye have a young Virgin of fifteen Years,
You must tickle her Fancy with sweets and dears,
Ever toying, and playing, and sweetly, sweetly,
Sing a Love Sonnet, and charm her Ears:
Wittily, prettily talk her down,
Chase her, and praise her, if fair or brown,
Sooth her, and smooth her,
And teaze her, and please her,
And touch but her Smicket, and all's your own.
Do ye fancy a Widow well known in a Man?
With a front of Assurance come boldly on,
Let her rest not an Hour, but briskly, briskly,
Put her in mind how her Time steals on;
Rattle and prattle although she frown,
Rowse her, and towse her from Morn to Noon,
Shew her some Hour y'are able to grapple,
Then get but her Writings, and all's your own.
Do ye fancy a Punk of a Humour free,
That's kept by a Fumbler of Quality,
You must rail at her Keeper, and tell her, tell her
Pleasure's best Charm is Variety,
Swear her much fairer than all the Town,

Try her, and ply her when Cully's gone,
Dog her, and jog her,
And meet her, and treat her,
And kiss with two Guinea's, and all's your own.

235. YO HO

CHORUS: Get it in, get it out,
                        quit fuckin' about.
                        Yo ho, yo ho, yo ho.

I put my hand upon her toe, yo ho, yo ho,
I put my hand upon her toe, yo ho, yo ho,
I put my hand upon her toe she said,
"Hey rugger yer much too low."

I put my hand upon her knee, yo ho, yo ho,
I put my hand upon her knee, yo ho, yo ho,
I put my hand upon her knee, she said,
"Hey rugger quit teasin'me."

I put my hand upon her thigh, yo ho, yo ho,
I put my hand upon her thigh, yo ho, yo ho,
I put MY hand upon her thigh, she said,
"Hey rugger yer gettin' me high."

I put my hand upon her ear, yo ho, yo ho,
I put my hand upon her ear, yo ho, yo ho,
I put my hand upon her ear, she said,
"Hey rugger yer not even there."

I put my hand upon her nose, yo ho, yo ho,
I put my hand upon her nose, yo ho, yo ho,
I put my hand upon her nose, she said,
"Hey rugger gimme that hose."

I put my hand upon her mouth, yo ho, yo ho
I put my hand upon her mouth, yo ho. yo ho.

I put my hand upon her mouth, she said,
"Hey rugger start headin' south."

I put my hand upon her tit, yo ho, yo ho,
I put my hand upon her tit, yo ho, yo ho,
I put my hand upon her tit, she said,
"Hey rugger that's not quite it."

I put my hand upon her twat, yo ho, yo ho,
I put my hand upon her twat, yo ho, yo ho,
I put my hand upon her twat, she said,
"Hey rugger now that's the spot."

I put my dick into her mouth, yo ho, yo ho,
I put my dick into her month, yo ho, yo ho,
I put my dick into her mouth, she said,
"Mmmmmmmugh ... Mmmmmmmugh ... Mmmmugh."

And now she lies in a pinewood box, yo ho, yo ho,
And now she lies in a pinewood box, yo ho, yo ho,
And now she lies in a pinewood box, she sucked
Too many rugger cocks.

They dug her up and fucked her again, yo ho, yo ho,
They dug her up and fucked her again, yo ho, yo ho,
They dug her up and fucked her again, and again,
And again, and again, and again.

236. YOU EXPECT ME

FOR MEN TO SING:

You expect me to get down on my hands and knees
And eat your pussy like a rat eats cheese
Well, I like cheese but I ain't no rat
And I like pussy but not like that
Your drawers may be clean and trimmed in lace

But you'll never, ever, ever sit your lily white ass on this poor boy's face
And I wouldn't lie to you
Not one pound

FOR WOMEN TO SING:

You expect me to get down on my hands and knees
And lick your boner 'cause you want me to please
Well, I like boners that are big and fat
And I'd never eat a boner that looked like that
Your prick may be slick and ready to cream
But the closest you'll ever, ever, ever get to me is a good wet dream
And I wouldn't lie to you
Not one pound

237. YOUNG COLLIN, CLEAVING OF A BEAM

Young *Collin*, cleaving of a Beam,
At ev'ry Thumping, thumping blow cry'd hem;
And told his Wife, and told his Wife,
And told his Wife who the Cause would know,
That Hem made the Wedge much further go:
Plump *Joan*, when at Night to Bed they came,
And both were Playing at that same;
Cry'd Hem, hem, hem prithee, prithee, prithee *Collin* do,
If ever thou lov'dst me, Dear hem now;
He laughing answer'd no, no, no,
Some Work will Split, will split with half a blow;
Besides now I Bore, now I bore, now I bore,
Now, now, now I bore,
I Hem when I Cleave, but now I Bore.

238. YOUNG ROGER OF KILDARE

Oh, mother, mother, dear
May I go to the fair
May I go with young Roger
Young Roger of Kildare
For I know he's kind and gentle
And will love me for my sake
And I know he will not harm me
Coming home from the wake.

Oh, daughter, daughter, dear
You may go to the fair
You may go with young Roger
Young Roger of Kildare
For I know he's kind and gentle
And will love you for your sake
But keep you legs close together
Coming home from the wake.

So she went to the fair
So she went to the fair
She went with young Roger
Young Roger of Kildare
So he stuffed her up with ice-cream
And he stuffed her up with cake
And he stuffed it right up her
Coming home from the wake.

239. YOUR SPOONING DAYS

Your spooning days are over,
Your pilot light is out,
What used to be your sex appeal
Is now your water spout.

You used to be embarrassed
To make the thing behave,

For every blooming morning
It would stand up and watch you shave.

But now. you are growing old,
It sure gives you the blues,
To see the thing hand down your leg,
And watch you shine your shoes.

240. YOU'RE A GRAND OLD FAG

(Sung to the tune of "Grand Old Flag")

You're a grand old fag,
And your wrinkled balls sag,
Your performance gets worse everyday.
You're an argument,
for abstinence,
A broomstick would be a better lay.
Every heart fears doom,
When you walk into the room,
Cause we've heard of your infamous fame,
Your limp old cock won't be forgot,
Cause we all know that you are lame.

Well you have no lust,
And your humps have no thrust,
You're a sad, sad excuse for a stud.
You should just give up,
Cause you can't get it up,
I think I would rather eat mud.
Well your body's rank,
And the tiger in your tank,
Is as dead as the rhythm you beat,
Cause we know the way that you perform,
You remind us of a creampuff in heat.

END

www.ingramcontent.com/pod-product-compliance
Lightning Source LLC
Chambersburg PA
CBHW051816090426

42736CB00011B/1501